SPECTRUM OF LOVE: MY JOURNEY THROUGH AUTISM

DR. SIMBI ANIMASHAUN

Published by **Horizon Over the Spectrum, Inc.**
P.O. Box 402
Redan, Georgia 30074

The Spectrum of Love: My Journey Through Autism is written by Dr. Simbi Animashaun and published under Horizon Over the Spectrum, Inc., a non-profit organization dedicated to promoting autism awareness and supporting children with autism, ages 2 to 14, and their families. The organization emphasizes serving Black families and underserved communities.

This book is a work of nonfiction. Events and experiences are recounted to the best of the author's memory. Some names and identifying details have been changed to protect privacy. **Disclaimer**: *The information in this book is for educational purposes only and should not be considered medical or legal advice.*

ISBN 979-8-9928596-0-7 (Paperback)
ISBN 979-8-9928596-1-4 (Hardcover)

Printed in the United States of America.
For more information, visit www.horizonsoverthespectrum.com

DEDICATION

First and foremost, I dedicate this memoir to my exceptional children, Messiah, Marjaani, Micah, and Malakai, whose courage, resilience, and unique brilliance inspire me daily. You have taught me to see the world in colors I never knew existed. This memoir is a testament to the love and lessons you have given me. This is for you, always!

To my kid's father, Maurice Payne, who taught me the meaning of unconditional love and has supported me through every trial I have experienced.

To every parent on this autism journey, may this memoir be your guide, companion, and source of hope.

TABLE OF CONTENTS

Acknowledgments vii

Introduction ix

Part 1: The Diagnosis – A New Chapter Begins
Chapter 1: Seeing the Signs 2
Chapter 2: The Day Everything Changed 9
Chapter 3: What Does Autism Mean for Our Family? 17

Part 2: Growing Together on the Spectrum
Chapter 4: Learning to See Through Their Eyes 25
Chapter 5: Celebrating Small Victories 34
Chapter 6: The Challenges We Face 37

Part 3: Building a Village 42
Chapter 7: Finding Allies 43
Chapter 8: Advocating for Your Child 53
Chapter 9: Leaning on Other Parents 58

Part 4: A Spectrum of Emotions 63
Chapter 10: The Highs and Lows 64
Chapter 11: Parenting with Resilience 76
Chapter 12: Love Without Limits 85

Part 5: Looking Toward the Future 93
Chapter 13: Supporting Their Independence 94
Chapter 14: Dreaming Big, Adjusting Wisely 103
Chapter 15: Embracing the Spectrum of Love 112

Conclusion: A Letter to My Children 119
    Final Words of Encouragement and Solidarity
    for Other Parents...121

Resources and Tools 123
    Tips for Starting Conversations about Autism
    with Others 124
    Recommended Books, Apps, and Tools for Parents
    and Kids.. 128
    A List of National and Local Autism Support
    Organizations...133

Glossary...137
References 144
About the Author..146
Contact Us..147

ACKNOWLEDGMENTS

This book would not have been possible without so many people's love, support, and inspiration. First, to the families of children with autism, especially those navigating the early days of a diagnosis: Your strength, resilience, and unwavering dedication to your children are the heart of this work. Thank you for sharing your stories and trusting us to help carry your voices.

To my family and friends, thank you for believing in this mission and supporting me every step of the way. Your encouragement and understanding gave me the strength to bring this project to life.

To the incredible professionals, educators, and advocates who are tirelessly working to create a more inclusive world, thank you for your guidance and expertise. Your insights shaped the content of this book and will empower countless families.

To the community served by Horizon Over the Spectrum, Inc., you are the reason we do this work. Your courage, determination, and love for your children inspire us daily.

Finally, this book is for everyone who has ever felt unseen or unheard in their journey with autism. I hope these pages bring you comfort, knowledge, and the reassurance that you are never alone.

With gratitude,
Dr. Simbi Animashaun
Co-Founder & Advocate, Horizon Over the Spectrum, Inc.

INTRODUCTION

Since I was a little girl, I always dreamed of being a mother. I would play "house" with my dolls and pretend to care for them like I thought a mother should. I named them Simeon (son) and Simone (daughter). They were my imaginary children. Parenting included bathing, feeding them breakfast, lunch, and dinner, reading books, combing their hair, and then tucking them tightly into bed at night. As I got older, my perspective on parenthood changed, and I eventually discovered that parenthood included a plethora of roles and responsibilities.

Eventually, my dream would become a reality in January 2014 when I discovered I was pregnant. I was 29 and a six-year middle school English teacher in the Metro Atlanta. I was excited about this new journey. I had been working with children to fulfill my desire for parenthood. I took my job very seriously. Unfortunately, my dreams were shattered when I experienced a miscarriage a few weeks after my first OB/GYN visit. If you've never experienced a miscarriage, let me share that it is one of the most painful and traumatic experiences. I had to deliver a dead fetus. A lack of support from the hospital staff, family, and friends drove me into depression that I eventually managed to overcome. I wrote about my experiences with recurrent miscarriages in my first published novel, *The Power of Healing: A Memoir of Loss & Victory*.

Two years later, I finally became a mother, unprepared for my life's new challenges. I would not only become a mother, but I would explore the parenthood of children on the autism spectrum. I must admit this journey has been a challenging yet rewarding experience. I have learned that love grows in every shade. Today, I am a mother of four beautiful blessings. My oldest children were both medically diagnosed with autism. In this parent guidebook, I offer hope, my personal experience parenting a child on the autism spectrum, and lessons learned for parents navigating similar journeys.

PART 1

THE DIAGNOSIS –
A NEW CHAPTER BEGINS

CHAPTER 1

SEEING THE SIGNS

My first son, Messiah, was born on January 18, 2018. After suffering multiple miscarriages, it was such a refreshing experience to give birth to him despite having a challenging pregnancy. At the beginning of my pregnancy, I worried every single day that I would lose him, but the anxiety decreased as I approached my delivery date. During my second trimester, I began to bleed heavily for days, but my OB/GYN assured me that everything was fine.

To comfort me, I had an ultrasound completed every 2-4 weeks. Hearing my son's heartbeat each time helped relieve the stress tremendously. In my third trimester, I began to show signs of pre-eclampsia. After a visit to the doctor's office, my blood pressure was 180/95, and they were unable to stabilize it that day. Thus, the surgeons moved my scheduled c-section surgery date up to the next day. I should have known something was wrong days before my doctor's visit because my feet were swollen, and I didn't have an appetite. Thankfully, I had no complications with surgery, and Messiah was a healthy 5 lb. and 12 oz. baby boy.

As a first-time mother, I would learn so much about a child's developmental stages even though I studied education in college and was a teacher. The first 4 months of his life were difficult. In addition to experiencing postpartum depression, I had a colicky new baby. He would cry from sun up to sun down for no apparent reason, and nothing seemed to work. These intensive crying episodes typically last three hours to three days, most weeks. His father, Daddy, and I tried everything! First, we changed his formula at least three times and hoped to find a sensitive brand to alleviate the gas and bloating. We also played white noise, rubbed his belly throughout the day, and gave him colic drops as needed. Despite being colicky, he met his developmental milestones each time we visited his pediatrician.

When he turned 6 months old, the colicky episodes drastically disappeared; I felt like I finally had a "normal" baby. *Let me add I intensively despise the word "normal" because it is used to ostracize those individuals who are uniquely different.* Messiah crawled, responded to his name, laughed, and danced when Daddy played his favorite songs, ate fruits and veggies, etc. Luther Vandross was Daddy's favorite music artist to play at 3 a.m. He was such a delightful baby. Always smiling and always laughing. He enjoyed playtime with his father, which consisted of Daddy chasing him around the house.

As time passed, he was still making adequate developmental progress at each visit to the pediatrician. By 10 months, he had learned to walk and had said "mama" and "dada." I also started teaching him his ABCs and 123s, and I was happy to hear him mimic words and sounds that he would hear me say. On the other hand, I failed to recognize some critical signs due to my demanding job, and at the time, his father and I were experiencing some challenges in our relationship. We would eventually separate and move into different households, but we learned to co-parent effectively for the sake of our children.

By this time, I had enrolled him in a new daycare closer to my job. Things were falling into place in our new home and daycare. Then, life drastically changed for us. I started receiving daily reports that often stated that Messiah had a difficult day, including biting the teachers and other children in the classroom, not responding when his name was called or "ignoring his teachers," not following simple directions, struggling to hold a fork, spoon, drink out of an open cup, and he often got hurt while there. I remember receiving a phone call that he had fallen into the bookshelf because he was running in the classroom and not listening to directions. This situation was shocking, but I blamed it on him undergoing "toddler blues."

On January 18, 2019, we celebrated his 1st birthday with a "Boss Baby" themed party at Catch Air. We had a blast with family and friends, and it was a joy to know I had survived my first year as a mother. I was very proud of myself. At his 12-month doctor's visit, he passed all of his developmental milestones. I shared his teacher's behavior concerns at that appointment, but Dr. B ignored me. Months later, I found out that I was pregnant with my daughter, and it seemed like my maternal instincts elevated. I began to notice that Messiah's development was regressing at 15 months. He stopped responding to his name and making eye contact when spoken to, saying "mama" and "dada," and his behavior worsened at his daycare. Unfortunately, most of my time was spent ensuring that I had a healthy pregnancy and delivery with my daughter.

Due to my age and medical history, I was deemed "high risk," and I was seeing different doctors, including a fetal and maternal specialist, every 2 weeks. This situation put an emotional and mental strain on me, especially since his father and I were still separated. By Christmas that year, we had moved into a newly purchased townhome, he was attending a new daycare, and his sister was born on November 1. I was now a single mother trying to balance two young children, a home, and a full-time job.

At the new daycare, Messiah's behavior worsened. He started eloping, running out of the classroom, laughing when being redirected by his teacher, being disruptive during learning time, etc. One day, the daycare's Director called and asked if I could pick him up. She shared that he had a tantrum and ran under her desk, and she could not control him. I immediately shared the news with my Assistant Principal, and on the way to pick him up, I cried because I knew something was wrong with him. I felt like it was my fault.

I had neglected him and not advocated for his needs. While waiting in the Director's office, the daycare's Head Cook stopped me and blatantly asked if he had gotten his autism diagnosis yet. I almost cursed her out. I was utterly shocked that she would say that to me, but instead of being rude, I asked her to explain her reason for saying that. She then went into detail about her eldest son and how she experienced similar situations when he was younger, later discovering that he was on the spectrum. I did not know much about autism other than my experiences with teaching children on the autism spectrum in my classroom, but this was very different.

When the Director entered the office, she shared behavior observations that the teacher had noticed about Messiah since joining her class. He often engaged in repetitive behaviors, such as fixating on spinning a toy car's wheels in the classroom. Messiah also had difficulty sitting in his chair during lessons and, as I mentioned before, would elope out of the classroom. Finally, she shared that he would not play with the other children and had difficulty with transitions. This instance was the primary reason for his meltdown. They were transitioning from one activity to another. When he joined us in the office, he acted as if nothing had happened. He ran and gave me a big hug.

That night, I cried again! The conversation with the Director and Head Cook played in my head repeatedly. I opened my laptop and began to research early signs of autism. My mouth dropped as I read several online articles. This research article described my son perfectly, from the lack of eye contact to delayed speech. How did

I miss this? The next day at work, I shared my concerns with a few coworkers, and they offered their advice. Attempting to balance my intuition and external advice as a parent was difficult. To be honest, I did not want to have a son on the autism spectrum or special needs. Motherhood instantly changed, and I was about to prepare for a new testament in my life.

Here are some common early signs of autism to look out for in children, typically noticeable by the age of 2–3 years:

Social Communication Signs:
— Limited Eye Contact
— Avoids or makes little eye contact during interactions

Delayed or Limited Speech:
— Do not babble or use single words by expected milestones
— Speech develops later or not at all in some cases

Difficulty Responding to Name:
— They may not respond when their name is called, even if they have normal hearing

Challenges with Social Interaction:
— Prefers to play alone rather than engage with peers or siblings
— Limited interest in social games like peek-a-boo

Unusual Tone of Voice:
— Speaks in a monotone or singsong voice or may repeat phrases without understanding (echolalia)

Behavioral Signs:
— Repetitive Behaviors
— Engages in repetitive actions like hand-flapping, rocking, spinning, or lining up toys

Restricted Interests:
- Shows intense focus on specific objects or activities (e.g., spinning wheels on a toy car)

Rigid Routines:
- Becomes upset by small changes in routines or surroundings

Difficulty with Transitions:
- Struggles to shift from one activity to another, sometimes leading to meltdowns

Sensory Processing Differences:
- Sensory Sensitivities
- Overly sensitive to sounds, lights, textures, or smells (e.g., covering ears, avoiding specific clothing)

Unusual Sensory Interests:
- Fascinated by sensory input, such as watching lights spin or feeling specific textures

Developmental Delays or Differences:
- Delayed Motor Skills
- May have difficulty with fine or gross motor skills (e.g., clapping, crawling, or walking)

Regression of Skills:
- Loss of previously acquired speech, social, or motor skills around 18–24 months

Unusual Play Patterns:
- Plays with toys in unconventional ways (e.g., lining them up instead of playing pretend)

Emotional or Behavioral Challenges:
– Difficulty Expressing Emotions
– Struggles to communicate emotions or understanding of others

Unusual Attachment to Objects:
– They may carry specific objects everywhere or become fixated on unusual items

Meltdowns or Tantrums:
– Intense emotional outbursts that are difficult to calm and often tied to frustration or sensory overload

Next Steps if You Notice Early Signs of Autism:
– Talk to Your Pediatrician: Share your observations and request a developmental screening.
– Request an Evaluation: An autism assessment can be conducted by Early Intervention (ages 0–3) or a developmental psychologist.
– Trust Your Intuition: If you feel something is different, seek professional guidance even if others advise waiting.

CHAPTER 2

THE DAY EVERYTHING CHANGED

After the incident at Messiah's daycare, I immediately shifted my attention to advocating for my son to receive the needed support. I called and scheduled an appointment with his pediatrician for the following week. I reiterated the behavior concerns I shared during his last developmental assessment appointment. His pediatrician started to assess him, and his opinion changed immediately.

He noticed the lack of eye contact, delayed speech, and that he was not responding to his name. He also observed Messiah being unable to sit still for the check-up. He had another meltdown in the patient room for about 10 minutes. His pediatrician then shared that those were clear signs of autism.

He referred us to our county's early intervention program. The program is called Babies Can't Wait. Dr. B also submitted an autism evaluation recommendation to the Marcus Autism Center. A caseworker from Babies Can't Wait contacted me the next day to explain the services offered and to get us enrolled in the program. Although I was overwhelmed with all this new information, I was excited that my child would receive early intervention services. Our casework was lovely, and she patiently empathized with me. We were also added to the waitlist at the Marcus Autism Center, where most parents are not contacted until 6 months to a year after a referral has been made.

Babies Can't Wait is Georgia's early intervention program for infants and toddlers (birth to 3 years old) with developmental delays or disabilities. It provides services to help children reach developmental milestones and support their families in addressing their unique needs. Here are key features of Babies Can't Wait:

Who Is Eligible?
— Age: Infants and toddlers from birth to 36 months.
— Developmental Delays: Children showing delays in areas such as communication, motor skills, social-emotional development, cognitive abilities, or adaptive/self-help skills.
— Diagnosed Conditions: Children with specific conditions known to result in developmental delays, such as Down syndrome, autism, or cerebral palsy.

Available Services:
— Developmental evaluations and assessments.
— Speech therapy, occupational therapy, and physical therapy.
— Special instruction and early learning strategies.
— Family training, counseling, and support.
— Service coordination to help families access resources and navigate the system.

How It Works?
— Step 1: Referral: Parents, healthcare providers, or anyone involved with the child can refer them to BCW.
— Step 2: Evaluation: A team of professionals assesses the child to determine eligibility and needs.
— Step 3: Individualized Family Service Plan (IFSP): If eligible, an IFSP is created, outlining the child's goals and the services needed to meet those goals.
— Step 4: Service Delivery: Services are typically provided in the child's natural environment, such as the home or daycare.

Cost:
- Babies Can't Wait operates on a sliding fee scale, and many services are free for families. Medicaid, private insurance, and other resources may help cover costs.

Benefits:
- Supports early learning and development during a critical time in a child's growth.
- Empower parents and caregivers with strategies and resources to help their child thrive.

How to Contact Babies Can't Wait:
- Referral Hotline: Families or providers can call 1-800-229-2038 or contact their local BCW program office.
- Website: For more information, visit the <u>Babies Can't Wait section of the Georgia Department of Public Health website</u>.

While I waited to be contacted by the Marcus Autism Center, Messiah received a developmental evaluation, and the results determined that he was eligible for BCW service because he had delays in his cognitive, communication, social-emotional, and self-help abilities. Thus, we drafted an Individual Family Service Plan (IFSP) and outlined goals and the services needed to meet his goals, such as speech and occupational therapy.

The following year, he received speech and occupational therapy twice a week. We also celebrated his 2nd birthday in January of 2020 at Hippo Hop. With this new information, I understood why he preferred to play alone and did not interact with his peers. At his party, he played by himself most of the time. In the party room, he covered his ears as we sang "Happy Birthday." I was glad that no one asked any questions because I just needed a break from thinking about autism for a moment. It had been difficult explaining to his father that he may have a child on the autism spectrum. He had blamed "vaccinations" on his potential autism diagnosis.

Unexpectedly, in February 2020, I discovered I was pregnant again! Also, the world was entering a severe pandemic caused by COVID-19. This news was devastating as I was finally finding a balance between work and home life, including getting Messiah the support he needed through speech and occupational therapy. COVID-19 caused us to enter into an isolation that negatively impacted his progression. Both speech and occupational therapy were put on hold. The only place that I was allowed to go was to my doctor's appointments. The kid's father ensured he supplied us with necessities like food, clothing, medications, etc.

Around June 2020, both kids received speech and occupational therapy as we began navigating the new norm. "Masks" and "social distancing," as government officials recommended, are the rules we followed. We wore masks when our speech and occupational therapists visited us for in-home services. Despite speech and occupational therapy, Messiah was not making adequate progress.

My second son, Micah, was born on November 2, 2020. Finally, in December, I received a call from the Marcus Autism Center to schedule his initial evaluation. With my son about to be evaluated, I began to observe similar early autism signs in his sister, Marjaani, so I contacted my BCW caseworker and had her evaluated. Simultaneously, I took Messiah to the Marcus Autism Center to be assessed and set up an appointment to get Marjaani evaluated with BCW.

A few weeks later, I received Messiah's diagnosis. He met the criteria for a diagnosis of Autism Spectrum Disorder (ASD), and implementing behavioral therapy through Applied Behavior Analysis was recommended to work on social engagement, following directions, safety awareness, flexibility, functional and cooperative play, and tantrums. He also met the criteria for mixed receptive-expressive language disorder, given his delays in both understanding and expression of speech. The psychologist also recommended speech therapy to continue working on vocalizations, gestures, and forming words.

The following week, he turned 3 years old, and we would proceed with a comprehensive psychoeducational evaluation through Dekalb County School District (DCSD) for placement in a specialized preschool program focusing on building his language and social skills. I felt relieved to receive his official medical diagnosis finally, but then I felt a bit of sadness that I did not get him the help he needed sooner. While balancing my new reality, I had to grieve expectations for my newly diagnosed son. At the same time, I had to mentally, emotionally, and physically prepare myself for having two children on the autism spectrum. My daughter also met eligibility to receive early intervention services with BCW.

Grieving expectations while embracing a new reality is a profound and deeply personal process that many parents go through when their child is diagnosed with autism or any condition that alters the vision they have for their child's future. It's a balancing act of honoring your emotions while finding the strength to move forward with love, acceptance, and hope. Honestly, I had to relearn how to be a mother to my son. I grieved for the son I thought I gave birth to - one who would be my scholar at school (making the honor roll every semester) or be the football star. It hurt, but I had to let go of that dream.

Although my dreams were shattered, Messiah opened my eyes to a new profound love of nature, technology, and laughing at silly movies. He taught me to celebrate every milestone and not sweat the small stuff. It warms my heart today when he runs off the bus and hugs me after being at school all day. Or when he wakes up and says, "Good Morning." Lately, he has been telling me, "I Love You!" Finally, he has taught me that success does not mean fitting into society's standards but embracing our differences and being ourselves! Here are some key insights and strategies for navigating this journey:

Allow Yourself to Grieve:
- Grief doesn't mean you're giving up on your child. It's a natural response to losing the expectations and dreams you may have held for their future.
- Recognize the Loss: It's okay to mourn milestones or paths you imagined, like traditional education or independence.
- Validate Your Feelings: Feelings of sadness, fear, guilt, or anger are normal. Grieving helps make space for healing and acceptance.
- Be Patient with Yourself: Grief is not linear. Some days may feel more challenging than others, and that's okay.

Shift Perspectives on Success:
- Reframe success not as a predefined path but as progress unique to your child's abilities and strengths.
- Celebrate Progress: Every milestone, no matter how small, is a victory worth celebrating.
- Define New Dreams: Focus on what makes your child happy and fulfilled rather than societal expectations.
- Appreciate the Present: Let go of the pressure to constantly look ahead and instead enjoy the unique joy your child brings to your life today.

Cultivate Acceptance:
- Acceptance doesn't mean giving up hope—it means embracing the child you have and supporting them as they are.

- Understand Autism as a Spectrum: Recognize that autism is not a tragedy but a different way of experiencing the world.
- Focus on Strengths: Learn about your child's unique gifts and passions, and let them guide your parenting.
- Practice Self-Compassion: Accept that you won't always have the answers, and that's okay.

Build Your Support System:
- Surround yourself with people who understand and uplift you.
- Connect with Other Parents: Support groups or online communities can provide empathy, advice, and camaraderie.
- Lean on Professionals: Therapists, counselors, and autism specialists can offer practical and emotional support.
- Educate Your Network: Help friends and family understand autism to support you and your child better.

Transform Guilt into Advocacy:
Parents often experience guilt, questioning if they could have done something differently. Shift this energy into becoming an advocate for your child.
- Learn and Empower Yourself: Understand your child's needs and rights to navigate education and therapies better.
- Advocate with Love: Be the voice for your child in schools, healthcare settings, and the community.
- Focus on Positives: Instead of dwelling on what could have been, channel energy into supporting your child's growth.

Embrace Your Child's Unique Journey:
Your child's path may look different from what you imagined, but it is filled with beauty and meaning.
- Redefine Joy: Find joy in moments of connection, learning, and love.
- Grow Alongside Your Child: Your child's journey will teach you patience, resilience, and the power of unconditional love.

- Celebrate the Spectrum of Love: Let your lover child guide you as you navigate this new reality.

Seek Hope and Inspiration:
- Read Stories of Other Families: Hearing how others have navigated their journeys can be uplifting.
- Focus on the Future: While the challenges are real, many children on the autism spectrum thrive in their unique ways with the proper support.
- Remember the Possibilities: Your child is capable of growth, happiness, and love—just as they are.

CHAPTER 3

WHAT DOES AUTISM MEAN FOR OUR FAMILY?

I vividly remember sitting in Dr. Miller's office at the Marcus Autism Center and feeling like I was in a movie. Like Fat Albert, my reality turned into a world I was unprepared for. As Dr. Miller reviewed his scores, of course, I did not know what the hell she was talking about. But, I could dissect bits and pieces of the evaluation results. Cognition, motor and gross, social and emotional learning, and communication language were all familiar. For this parent guidebook, I want to be clear on how I unpacked my son's diagnosis and what that meant practically and emotionally for my family.

Based on the parental report, developmental testing, and previous evaluations, Messiah met the criteria for a diagnosis of mixed receptive and expressive language disorder and ASD. I was unfamiliar with mixed receptive and expressive language disorder. In my research over the years, I have learned that mixed receptive and expressive language disorder is a communication disorder in which a person has difficulty understanding spoken or written language (receptive skills) and expressing themselves effectively (expressive skills). It can affect vocabulary, grammar, sentence structure, and comprehension. This disorder is common in children on the autism spectrum or developmental delays but can also occur due to other factors, such as brain injuries or genetic conditions. Here are characteristics of Mixed Receptive and Expressive Language Disorder:

Receptive Challenges:
- Difficulty following directions.
- Struggles with understanding complex sentences or questions.
- Misinterpreting the meaning of words or phrases.

Expressive Challenges:
- Limited vocabulary or difficulty finding the right words.
- Trouble forming grammatically correct sentences.
- Difficulty telling stories or relaying information.

Social Impact:
- Challenges in conversations and peer interactions.
- Possible frustration or withdrawal due to communication struggles.

How Families Can Cope Emotionally
- Supporting a child with this disorder can be emotionally challenging, but here are ways families can manage:

Educate Yourself:
- Learn about the disorder to better understand your child's needs. Knowing the reasons behind their challenges can foster patience and empathy.

Build a Support System:
- Connect with other families who face similar challenges. Support groups or community organizations, like autism-focused nonprofits, can provide valuable advice and emotional support.

Work with Professionals:
- Partner with speech-language pathologists (SLPs) to create a personalized intervention plan for your child.

– Seek guidance from psychologists or therapists if feelings of stress, guilt, or frustration arise.

Celebrate Small Victories:
– Focus on and celebrate every progress your child makes, no matter how small. This helps to stay motivated and positive.

Communicate Openly as a Family:
– Share feelings and frustrations within your family. Let siblings express their feelings; they may also need reassurance and support.

Take Breaks:
– Caring for a child with communication challenges can be overwhelming. Practice self-care and lean on trusted family or friends when you need a break.

Advocate and Empower:
– Advocate for your child's needs at school or in therapy. At the same time, help them build confidence by teaching them alternative communication tools, such as visual aids or sign language.

On the other hand, ASD is broken down into two main components: social communication and repetitive behaviors/restrictive interests. As it related to social communication, evidence showed that Messiah had challenges consistently responding to his name, did not share interests nor initiate joint attention, did not offer comfort to others, displayed inconsistent eye contact and limited gesture language, lacked cooperative play skills, and did not respond to the social cues of others (often in his world).

Can you imagine the emotional state I was in as a parent, sitting in a small room with bright lights, listening to a doctor tell me all the things WRONG with my child? I was devastated. It did not stop there! Dr. Miller proceeded to share that Messiah displayed spinning, toe walking, hand flapping, lined-up toys, difficulty with transitions, a high tolerance for pain tolerance, and a fascination with watching objects spin. I thought to myself, *Goodness! I must be on the autism spectrum, too, because I remember exhibiting several of these characteristics as a child and adult.*

By the end of the 1-hour appointment, Dr. Miller began to provide the Recommendation Plan. At this point, I was ready to go home. My brain could not process any more information. She may have sensed my desire to leave because she rushed through the recommendations and asked if I had any questions. *No,* I responded. As I drove home, I continued to process my new reality. Both autism and mixed receptive and expressive language diagnosis can bring a mix of emotions. I felt relief, worry, uncertainty, and even hope.

Adjusting to this new reality as a family requires a strong sense of unity, understanding, and resilience. This new reality can look different for each family, so adjust according to the dynamics of your family. My other children were very young (3 under 3). To be honest, I was the only one impacted in my family as I was a single mother who had to adjust our sleep hygiene, nutrition, and feeding schedule, physical home space, including toy organization, colors, lighting, visual and auditory distractions, etc. (to avoid sensory overload). I also had to create an accommodating daily schedule to meet the needs of Messiah, including sensory breaks, ABA, speech, and occupational therapy. Here are some practical steps for finding strength together:

Take Time to Process the Diagnosis:
- Acknowledge Your Emotions: It's normal for family members to feel various emotions. Permit yourself to grieve the expectations you may have had, but also focus on embracing your child's unique qualities.
- Be Patient with Each Other: Everyone processes the diagnosis differently. Allow space for each family member to adjust at their own pace.

Learn Together:
- Educate Yourself: Knowledge is power. Read books, attend workshops, and connect with autism-focused organizations. Understanding autism helps dispel fears and uncertainties.
- Involve the Whole Family: Teach siblings and extended family members about autism in age-appropriate ways. This will build empathy and reduce misunderstandings.

Build a Support Network:
- Connect with Other Families: Join support groups for families of children on the autism spectrum. Sharing experiences with others who truly understand can be incredibly comforting.
- Rely on Professionals: Work closely with therapists, educators, and medical professionals to create a roadmap for your child's development. They can provide guidance tailored to your family's needs.

Create a Positive Family Culture:
- Focus on Strengths: Celebrate your child's unique abilities and achievements. Shifting the focus from challenges to strengths can foster a positive mindset.
- Practice Gratitude: Cultivate a sense of gratitude for the love and connection within your family. This can help ground you in difficult moments.

Maintain Open Communication:
- Share Your Feelings: Create a safe space for everyone in the family to express their thoughts, frustrations, or fears without judgment.
- Listen Actively: Validate each other's emotions and provide reassurance. This strengthens emotional bonds within the family.

Prioritize Self-Care for Everyone:
- Parents, you can't pour from an empty cup. Take time to recharge through exercise, hobbies, or connecting with friends.
- Siblings: Spend one-on-one time with siblings to ensure they don't feel overlooked. Address their feelings and encourage them to voice their needs.
- Extended Family: Include them in your support system, but don't hesitate to set boundaries if their reactions to the diagnosis aren't helpful.

Embrace a Team Mindset:
- Work Together: Involve all family members in supporting your child through social skills practice or therapy sessions. This will help everyone feel connected and involved.
- Be Flexible: Autism can bring unpredictable moments. Approach challenges as opportunities for growth and adapt together.

Focus on the Bigger Picture:
- Remember Your Child's Potential: Autism is a journey, not a limitation. Many children on the autism spectrum grow into happy, thriving adults with the proper support.
- Stay Hopeful: Trust that you can overcome obstacles and grow stronger together as a family.

Seek Professional and Emotional Support:
- Family Therapy: Counseling can help families process the diagnosis, address feelings of guilt or overwhelm, and build better communication strategies.
- Spiritual Support: If faith or spirituality is essential to your family, lean into those practices to find meaning, comfort, and hope.

Celebrate the Small Moments:
- Appreciate Progress: Every step forward, no matter how small, is a victory worth celebrating.
- Create Joyful Memories: Spend time together doing activities your child loves, strengthening bonds, and creating a positive family atmosphere.

Remember, strength doesn't mean never struggling; it means showing up for each other through the challenges. A family that works together to understand and support their child can become an unbreakable source of love, resilience, and encouragement. I often struggle to prioritize self-care, which I discuss further in Chapter 11.

I promote it to other mothers and families through my nonprofit organizations. I am the President and Chief Executive Officer of the United By Loss Foundation, Inc. in DeKalb County, GA. Our mission is to provide grief support, access to educational resources and tools, and advocacy for Black mothers and families impacted by pregnancy and infant loss. I also recently co-founded another nonprofit organization with my kid's father, Horizon Over the Spectrum, Inc., which will focus on providing support to underserved Black families impacted by ASD. This parent guidebook will serve as one of our initial resources for families.

PART 2

GROWING TOGETHER
ON THE SPECTRUM

CHAPTER 4

LEARNING TO SEE THROUGH
THEIR EYES

After I received Messiah's official Autism diagnosis, he turned 3 years old. He was evaluated to see if Dekalb County Public School could serve him in a special education preschool class. The evaluation was a smooth process as the COVID-19 pandemic was still present. I don't even think we celebrated his birthday that year because I had to prepare him to start preschool at our local elementary school the following week. Of course, the school would be virtual. He would transition into the preschool class at Flat Rock Elementary School.

In addition, I was still teaching myself. I was a 7th-grade English teacher at Cedar Grove Middle School. I had to learn how to balance work, school for Messiah, and my other children in the household.

Trying to understand Messiah's unique way of perceiving the world was challenging. He loved technology and could navigate a laptop or tablet better than most adults. He also was fascinated with twirling pieces of string and paper. What I deemed as "weird" was interesting. I had to learn to see through my child's eyes to understand him better and be a good parent. This included shifting my perspective to understand Messiah's way of experiencing the world so that I could connect with him on a deeper level, foster trust, and celebrate his individuality. Here are strategies to help you on this journey:

Observe Without Judgment:
- Spend time quietly watching how your child interacts with their environment.
- Notice what they're drawn to, how they process sensory input, and what brings them joy.
- Avoid interpreting behaviors based on typical expectations; ask yourself what those behaviors might mean for your child. For example, if your child enjoys spinning objects, see it as their way of exploring patterns or regulating their sensory input rather than focusing on it as "different" or "unusual."

Tune Into Their Sensory World:
Children on the autism spectrum often have unique sensory sensitivities or preferences. Understanding these differences can help you empathize and adapt.
- Over-Sensitivity: Bright lights, loud noises, or certain textures might feel overwhelming.
- Under-Sensitivity: They may seek sensory input through movement, touch, or sound to feel grounded.

How to Try:
- Spend a few minutes in a busy, loud place and imagine how that might feel if your senses were heightened.
- Experiment with textures, sounds, and lights to see what your child gravitates toward or avoids.

Communicate on Their Term:
If verbal communication is challenging, embrace their unique ways of expressing themselves.
- Use gestures, facial expressions, or visual aids to communicate.
- Learn their "language"—whether it's a specific way they point, repeat phrases, or express emotions through stimming (repetitive behaviors like hand-flapping or rocking).

— Celebrate small connections, such as shared eye contact or a smile. If they show you an object instead of using words, acknowledge their effort by enthusiastically engaging with it: "You're showing me your favorite toy! Tell me more about it."

Engage in Their Interests:
Children on the autism spectrum often have intense, focused interests. Instead of redirecting them, join them in their passions.

— Take time to learn about what they love: training, animals, numbers, or a specific cartoon.

— Use these interests as a bridge to teach new skills or build connections. Example: If your child loves dinosaurs, use dinosaur-themed activities to practice counting, reading, or social interactions.

Slow Down and Follow Their Lead:
Children on the autism spectrum may have their own pace and rhythm for exploring the world.

— Avoid rushing or imposing your agenda; let them guide the interaction.

— Be patient during transitions or new activities. Example: If your child spends a long time lining up toys, resist interrupting them. Instead, join in by lining up toys alongside them, showing that you value their way of playing.

Understand Emotional Expressions:
Children on the autism spectrum may express emotions differently. Meltdowns, for example, are often a result of sensory overload, frustration, or difficulty communicating.

— Recognize the underlying cause of their behavior rather than viewing it as "misbehavior."

— Provide calming tools like noise-canceling headphones, weighted blankets, or quiet spaces to help them regulate emotions. For example, if your child is upset after a noisy event, validate their feelings by saying, "I know it was loud, and that felt uncomfortable. Let's take a break together."

Learn Through Play:
Play is a powerful way to connect and understand how your child sees the world.
– Enter their world by playing how they play, even if it's different from typical games.
– Use imaginative play or sensory activities to build communication and trust. For example, if your child loves spinning, spin with them! This shared experience can strengthen your bond and help you understand their joy.

Educate Yourself About Autism:
– Read books, watch videos, or attend workshops to deepen your understanding of autism.
– Seek out resources written by individuals on the autism spectrum to gain firsthand insight into their experiences. Remember, autism isn't a deficit; it's a different way of processing and interacting with the world.

Ask for Help:
– Work with therapists or specialists who can guide you in understanding your child's unique needs.
– Connect with other parents or adults on the autism spectrum for advice and perspective.

See the Beauty in Their Perspective:
– Let go of preconceived ideas of what life "should" look like and embrace your child's unique lens on the world.
– Appreciate the joy they find in patterns, their incredible focus on details, and their authenticity in expressing emotions. Example: If your child notices the tiniest cracks on the

sidewalk, see it as an opportunity to marvel at their incredible attention to detail and curiosity about their surroundings.

Seeing through the eyes of a child on the autism spectrum is an opportunity to broaden your perspective and deepen your understanding of the world. It requires patience, openness, and a willingness to step outside your viewpoint. But in doing so, you'll discover the beauty, wonder, and love that makes their world unique.

For the next few months, as Messiah attended school, I learned a lot about autism, including stimming. Stimming (short for self-stimulatory behavior) refers to repetitive actions, movements, or sounds that individuals—especially those on the autism spectrum—use to regulate their emotions, sensory input, or focus. Stimming is a natural part of how many people on the autism spectrum interact with their environment and process information. Messiah enjoyed spinning in circles. Before his diagnosis, I would yell at him to stop and go sit down. But I embraced it now. Sometimes, I would join him in spinning in circles, making him so happy. We would spring until we got dizzy and fell on the floor.

In some cases, I would make him stop spinning because he was in a dangerous environment that could harm him. I recognized that he would stim (e.g., spin circles) to self-regulate when he was excited or seek additional stimulation when bored. Have you identified examples of stimming behaviors in your child yet? What do they enjoy doing? Here are some examples of stimming behaviors:

Physical Stimming:
- Hand-flapping
- Rocking back and forth
- Spinning in circles
- Jumping or bouncing

Auditory Stimming:
- Repeating certain sounds or phrases (echolalia)
- Humming or singing the same tune
- Making clicking, buzzing, or other vocal noises

Visual Stimming:
- Watching spinning objects (e.g., fans or wheels)
- Flicking fingers in front of the eyes
- Staring at patterns, lights, or reflections

Tactile Stimming:
- Touching or rubbing certain textures (e.g., soft fabrics, surfaces)
- Tapping or drumming fingers
- Repetitively running fingers through hair

Object-Based Stimming:
- Lining up or stacking objects
- Spinning toys or items like coins
- Fidgeting with objects (e.g., fidget spinners, stress balls)

Why Do People Stim?
Stimming serves various purposes and differs from person to person. Common reasons include:

Regulating Sensory Input:
To calm an overwhelmed sensory system or to seek additional stimulation in a sensory-deprived moment.
- Managing Emotions: To express excitement, happiness, anxiety, or frustration.
- Focusing or Blocking Distractions: To concentrate in challenging environments by redirecting focus to something predictable and comforting.
- Self-Soothing: To cope with stress, uncertainty, or sensory overload.

Is Stimming Harmful?

Most stimming behaviors are harmless and serve an essential self-regulatory function. In some cases, stimming may become unsafe or disruptive (e.g., head-banging or self-injury), in which case intervention strategies might be needed to replace it with safer alternatives.

Should Stimming Be Stopped?

Generally, stimming should not be discouraged unless it is harmful or disruptive to the individual or others. Instead of focusing on stopping stimming, consider:

- Understanding the Root Cause: Is the person overstimulated, anxious, or trying to self-regulate?
- Providing Support: Offer sensory tools, calming activities, or ways to address stress.
- Respecting Individual Differences: Stimming is a part of how many individuals on the autism spectrum express themselves and navigate their world.

How to Support Someone Who Stims?

- Create a Safe Environment: Allow stimming in comfortable spaces without judgment.
- Offer Alternatives (If Necessary): Provide tools like fidget toys or weighted blankets for additional sensory input.– Advocate for Acceptance: Help others understand that stimming is a natural and valuable behavior for many people on the autism spectrum.

Messiah enjoyed attending school every day. His preschool special education teacher, Ms. G, taught me a lot about my son. We immediately became friends as I appreciated her love and dedication to my son and all the students in her classroom. She was funny and attentive to her students' needs, and she provided lessons that engaged the students. Although Messiah struggled during instruction (due to his inattentiveness and hyperactivity), she still found a way to engage him. By April 2021, my son had made adequate progress in achieving his Individualized Education Plan (IEP) goals.

I had to understand the importance of empathy, patience, and flexibility. These qualities are foundational for supporting children on the autism spectrum because they create an environment that fosters trust, understanding, and growth. Here's why they are so important:

First, empathy allows caregivers, educators, and family members to view the world through the child's lens, understanding their unique experiences, challenges, and strengths. For children on the autism spectrum, sensory sensitivities, communication differences, or routines may feel overwhelming, and having someone acknowledge their feelings can provide comfort. Empathy also helps reduce frustration and ensures that children feel valued and respected. Here's how to practice empathy:

- Actively listen to what the child is communicating, verbally or nonverbally.
- Validate their emotions without judgment, even if you don't fully understand their perspective.
- Educate yourself on autism to better anticipate and respond to their needs.

Next, children on the autism spectrum often learn, communicate, and adapt at their own pace. Demonstrating patience provides them with the time and space they need to process situations, develop skills, and express themselves without pressure. Impatience can lead to stress and hinder progress, while patience encourages a sense of safety and support. Here's how to practice patience:

- Give them ample time to respond during conversations or activities.

- Celebrate small achievements instead of focusing solely on milestones.
- Manage your expectations and avoid comparisons with neurotypical peers.

Finally, flexibility is essential because children on the autism spectrum may have rigid preferences, routines, or responses to change. Adaptability helps them navigate unexpected situations while respecting their need for structure. Some children thrive with routines, but others may need creative approaches to engage with their surroundings. Here's how to practice flexibility:

- Modify your approach when something isn't working, whether communication, teaching, or play.
- Prepare for changes in routine by introducing them gradually or using visual aids to ease transitions.
- Respect their boundaries but remain open to trying new methods when needed.

CHAPTER 5

CELEBRATING SMALL VICTORIES

The end of the semester was slowly approaching its end. In May 2021, school ended, and I took Messiah and his siblings on an outing to celebrate. By this point, I had resigned from the DeKalb County School District. I was forced to resign, but that's another story in a different book. As local businesses slowly reopened, I was excited to take them to Catch Air for fun. As soon as I opened the doors, the kids ran into Catch Air with so much energy, and I did not care because they longed for socialization and a change in the environment.

I kept a close eye on them, especially Messiah because I did not know what to expect from him. We had not been confined to our home all year. Scanning the room, I wanted to ensure I had an eye on all my children. Marjaani was screaming as she slid down a slide. Micah interacted with other boys as they threw balls at an interactive game screen. Messiah, surprisingly, was helping a little girl who had fallen on the floor. My heart melted as I was in complete awe at his attention to help this little girl.

Typically, he would not respond if he saw another child falling or displaying sadness. I was so happy with his progress. I ran to him, hugged him, and told him a good job for being a good friend. Then, I offered him ice cream to celebrate such an incredible social skill milestone. That huge smile on his face informed me that he would accept my ice cream offer. On this day, I learned the importance of why progress matters more than perfection with children on the autism spectrum because their developmental journey is often unique, non-linear, and deeply personal. Here's why progress matters more:

Each autistic child develops at their own pace, and comparing them to neurotypical peers or aiming for "perfect" outcomes can be counterproductive. Progress, no matter how small, signifies meaningful growth. Recognizing and celebrating these steps fosters confidence and motivation for the child and their support network. For example, a child who makes eye contact briefly or learns a new word is making progress that can build a foundation for further development.

Additionally, striving for perfection often creates unrealistic expectations for the child, caregivers, and educators. This pressure can lead to frustration, anxiety, and burnout. When progress is the focus, it allows for more flexibility and fosters a positive atmosphere where the child feels supported, not judged. Key mindset shift: Perfection isn't the goal—growth, learning, and connection are.

Moreover, individuals on the autism spectrum have diverse strengths and challenges. Focusing on progress highlights what the child *can* do and how they improve, rather than fixating on their struggles. This approach builds self-esteem and encourages them to use their strengths meaningfully. For example, a child who struggles with verbal communication may excel at expressing themselves through art or technology. Progress can mean finding alternative ways to connect.

Progress emphasizes gradual, sustainable improvement that benefits the child long-term. Rushing to achieve "perfect" behaviors or skills may overlook the importance of building trust, emotional regulation, and independence in ways that respect their individuality. Why this matters: It's not about quickly hitting milestones but building a strong foundation for lifelong growth.

When caregivers and educators focus on progress, they create a supportive and encouraging environment. This strengthens the child's relationships with those around them as the emphasis shifts to celebrating achievements, fostering patience, and building mutual trust.

The goal is ultimately to help children on the autism spectrum thrive in their way, at their own pace. Perfection is an arbitrary and often unattainable standard, but progress—no matter how small—represents real and meaningful change. Every step forward is a success worth celebrating. That's exactly what I focused on in Summer 2021, including celebrating Messiah's progress, no matter how small.

CHAPTER 6

THE CHALLENGES WE FACE

During the summer, I decided to enroll Messiah in an ABA program. I did not want to take a break in getting him as much support as possible. I searched and searched online for days, completed intake forms, and finally received a response from an ABA company in the metro Atlanta area. Initially, the owner of the company was very nice.

During our first phone call, she explained her role and the process for enrolling Messiah in her program. She interviewed me, asking questions related to Messiah's autism diagnosis and the challenges he was facing at home and/or school. In addition to the parent interview, she evaluated him (in person) to determine his strengths and weaknesses. Then, she created a treatment plan based on the results. Similarly to his autism evaluation, he struggled with his expressive and receptive language, stimming, following directions, and self-care abilities, such as toileting and brushing his teeth.

To my knowledge, ABA therapy is a widely used intervention for individuals with ASD. Using evidence-based behavioral principles, it is designed to help develop skills, improve communication, enhance social interactions, and reduce challenging behaviors. Although there are success stories with ABA, I want to ensure I share our experiences with ABA and detailed information regarding the intervention. Every child on the autism spectrum is different. They have different needs. ABA was ineffective for Messiah, but because ABA therapy did not work for him does not mean it will not work for other children on the autism spectrum. Here's a closer look at ABA therapy, its benefits, and considerations:

ABA is a therapy rooted in behavioral science. It focuses on understanding how behavior works, how it is affected by the environment, and how learning occurs. Therapists use positive reinforcement to encourage desired behaviors and skills while reducing behaviors that may interfere with learning or daily life.

Key Components:
- Assessment: A comprehensive evaluation of the child's strengths, challenges, and goals.
- Individualized Treatment Plans: Goals are tailored to the child's needs and may include communication, social skills, self-care, and academics.
- Data-Driven Approach: Therapists collect data to track progress and adjust strategies as needed.
- Positive Reinforcement: Desired behaviors are rewarded to encourage repetition.

Benefits of ABA Therapy:
- Skill Development: ABA can help teach language, social interaction, self-care, and academic abilities.
- Behavior Management: Helps reduce challenging behaviors (e.g., aggression and self-injury) by teaching alternative, more adaptive behaviors.
- Improved Communication: ABA supports children in developing ways to express their needs verbally or nonverbally.
- Independence: ABA promotes independence over time by breaking down complex tasks into smaller, manageable steps.
- Customization: ABA is individualized, ensuring goals align with the child's abilities and family priorities.

While research widely supports ABA, it has also been criticized. Some individuals and families believe that specific approaches focus too heavily on compliance or suppressing natural behaviors, which can feel invalidating or stressful. Here are some common concerns:

- Focus on "normalization": Some argue that ABA prioritizes making children on the autism spectrum behave like neurotypical peers instead of celebrating their unique traits.
- Over-reliance on drills: Intensive, repetitive sessions may feel rigid or overwhelming for the child.
- Trauma Concerns: If done improperly, ABA may unintentionally lead to negative emotional experiences.

To ensure a positive experience:

- Child-Centered Goals: Goals should be meaningful to the child and their family, emphasizing quality of life over conformity.
- Compassionate Approach: ABA should be delivered with empathy, focusing on the child's strengths and respecting their individuality.
- Parental Involvement: Families should be actively involved in setting goals and learning techniques to support progress at home.
- Balanced Intensity: Therapy schedules should balance skill-building with downtime to prevent burnout.

Some families may choose to complement or explore alternatives to ABA, such as:
- Speech Therapy
- Occupational Therapy
- Developmental or Play-Based Therapies (e.g., DIR/Floortime)
- Social Skills Groups

ABA can be an effective tool for supporting children on the autism spectrum. Still, choosing a provider who aligns with your values and prioritizes your child's well-being is essential. When applied thoughtfully and with a child-centered focus, ABA can help children make meaningful progress while respecting their individuality. To reiterate, ABA was not an effective tool for Messiah. During the first few one-on-one sessions with the ABA therapist, her energy did not sit well with me. She did not embrace my thoughts and feelings regarding Messiah's treatment plan, which focused primarily on his meltdowns. Instead, her focus was getting him to conform to her rules and be "normal." Earlier in this parent guidebook, I shared my perspective on using that word. Immediately, I did not like her and requested a new ABA therapist. However, the company was short-staffed, and finding a replacement would take some time.

While we waited for a replacement, ABA sessions continued, and I made sure to monitor Messiah and the ABA therapist closely. One day, I heard him screaming upstairs. I ran upstairs to investigate the situation. He is nonverbal, so I always ran to his rescue to ensure he was not mistreated. When I asked why his meltdown was, she said, "I took his favorite toy and won't return it. It's supposed to teach him obedience." "OBEDIENCE!" I responded.

When I looked over at him, his face was completely red, and he was kicking my wall. "No, ma'am! I don't play that. He will not kick my walls. I just moved into this townhome, and he will respect it." I escorted her out of my home quickly and contacted her supervisor. Her supervisor apologized and begged me to give her another chance. Her final chance would be the next day. Of course, he had another meltdown, but instead of asking me for support to calm him down, she allowed him to draw on my carpet with his crayons. Words cannot express how upset I was. I politely told her that she could not return to my home.

That situation prepared me for trial and error in managing challenges. Managing challenges for children on the autism spectrum requires patience, creativity, and a willingness to adapt. Trial and error occurred when he returned to school in August 2021. He would be in the same class but face-to-face with the same teacher. However, the energy between Ms. G and I shifted as I noticed she mistreated my son. I also began to feel overwhelmed and unsure of how to navigate IEP meetings. In a professional setting, Ms. G was a bit aggressive, and at most times, I felt like she was not embracing my thoughts and opinions regarding Messiah's goals and progression.

After connecting with a parent mentor, I learned to document incidents that occurred at school and request specific accommodations to address his needs, such as sensory breaks and extra time on assignments. The last week before school ended for Winter Break, Ms. G called me to tell me that Messiah had an accident using the restroom and asked if I could bring some clothing to the school. Unfortunately, I could not, so I asked if she could check with the counseling department to see if they had any clothing.

I thought she had solved the problem until he got off the school bus that afternoon. She sent him on the bus in shorts. I was furious because it was December, and it was frigid outside. I spent that Christmas taking care of three sick children. When he returned to school from Winter Break, I strongly advocated for my son to navigate the school system appropriately. From that moment, I became the Autism Super Mom! The following semester, I documented everything, attended all meetings, and ensured that all teachers and staff heard my voice. This story highlighted the importance of trial and error, reaching out for support, and advocating for your child.

PART 3

BUILDING A VILLAGE

CHAPTER 7

FINDING ALLIES

Support systems are vital for families raising children on the autism spectrum, as they provide emotional strength, practical advice, and hands-on assistance in navigating the unique challenges of autism. Our support system included our speech-language pathologist, occupational therapist, and educators. They all contributed to the success of not only Messiah but his siblings as well. Earlier, I shared that Marjaani and Micah were showing signs of autism as well. By the Summer of 2022, all three of my children were receiving therapy from a speech-language pathologist and occupational therapist.

Our occupational therapist, Ms. Vanessa, became family. Initially, she was helping Messiah with sensory integration, motor skills, and daily living tasks, such as toileting, eating, and dressing. Then, she gradually started providing the same support to the other children. I don't think she knows the positive impact that she had on the children and me. She was such a nice person, and it was evident that she was knowledgeable, warm-hearted, and genuinely cared about the success of her clients. I enjoyed our conversations at the end of the children's sessions. Some days, she was scheduled to provide interventions to all three children, and it made my heart smile, as was how she catered to each child's needs. At that time, I did not have friends to talk to. I began to feel isolated, but Vanessa eased that feeling each time she visited us. She also taught me how to advocate for school accommodations, provided resources, and gave me hope, understanding, and a sense of belonging.

Messiah took a break from OT, and Marjaani and Micah graduated from the program because they had met or exceeded their goals. She eventually moved back to her hometown, Washington D.C. We miss her so much, but I know she's in D.C. making a difference in other children's lives. If it wasn't for Vanessa during this time in my life, I am most certain that I would have fallen into depression. Hopefully, your journey in finding a support system is different from mine. Here are additional elements of a support system to consider:

Therapists: Building Skills and Confidence—
Therapists, such as speech-language pathologists, occupational therapists, and behavior analysts, play a crucial role in helping children develop essential skills. For example:
–   Speech therapists work on communication skills through verbal language, alternative communication devices, or gestures.
–   Occupational therapists help children with sensory integration, motor skills, and daily tasks like dressing or eating.
–   Behavior therapists often use approaches like ABA (Applied Behavior Analysis) to reinforce positive behaviors and teach social or coping skills.

These professionals help children and empower parents with strategies they can use at home.

Educators: Advocates for Learning and Growth—
Teachers and special education professionals are key to creating an inclusive and supportive learning environment. They provide:
–   Individualized Education Plans (IEPs) are tailored to the child's specific needs, ensuring access to resources such as sensory tools, visual schedules, or modified assignments.
–   A sense of routine and predictability is often comforting for children on the spectrum.

– Advocacy within the school system, helping parents secure accommodations or additional support services.

Collaboration between educators and families ensures children have the best chance to succeed academically and socially.

Friends: A Network of Understanding—

Friends (both for the child and the parents) offer companionship and understanding that can ease feelings of isolation. For parents, friendships with other families raising children on the autism spectrum can be a lifeline. These connections can provide:

– Shared experiences, advice, and encouragement during tough times.
– Playdates or social opportunities for children on the autism spectrum help them practice interactions in a supportive environment.
– Emotional validation, as talking with someone who "gets it," can be deeply comforting.

Extended Family: A Bridge to Broader Inclusion—

Extended family members (like grandparents, aunts, and uncles) can play an important role when informed and supportive. They provide:

– Emotional support, showing parents they are not alone in their journey.
– Respite care offers breaks for parents to recharge, essential for avoiding burnout.
– Inclusion includes making family gatherings autism-friendly and ensuring the child feels welcome.
– Educating the extended family about autism helps them understand behaviors and offer constructive support rather than judgment.

The Broader Community: Building Acceptance—

Communities can foster understanding and acceptance beyond immediate family and professionals. Autism-friendly organizations, community programs, and neighbors who offer patience and kindness can reduce stigma and help families feel less isolated.

The Benefits of a Strong Support System:

- Emotional Well-being: Support systems remind families they don't have to face challenges alone, reducing feelings of stress and anxiety.
- Shared Knowledge: Collaborating with therapists, teachers, and friends provides access to tools, strategies, and resources.
- Improved Outcomes: When multiple people work together to meet a child's needs, the chances of success—whether in communication, social skills, or academics—increase significantly.

Support systems indeed reinforce the idea that "it takes a village" to help a child on the autism spectrum thrive. Who has been the most impactful part of your support network? Or is there an area where you'd like more support?

At that time, my support system was poor because I did not know how to navigate judgment and misunderstanding from others. We live in a world full of opinionated people who love offering advice, even if they have never experienced the situation. I remember picking Messiah up from school early one day and decided to take him for ice cream while the other children were in daycare. When we walked into the ice cream shop, he excitedly ran to the counter so that he could choose his flavor.

The employee, a young white male (*no older than 19*), began to ask Messiah questions: "Hey Buddy! What flavor do you think you want?" "Would you like toppings? We have over 20 toppings?" When Messiah did not respond, he looked at me confusingly and

46

asked, "Is he alright? Does he talk?" I had to explain to him that Messiah is non-verbal. "What does that mean?" he continued to ask. I do not think he was malicious, yet he was curious why Messiah could not talk. I explained to him that Messiah was diagnosed with autism at the age of 3 (now 5), and he has mixed expressive and receptive language disorder. "Oh, I heard that vaccines cause autism." I ended the conversation quickly because I wanted to enjoy this one-on-one time with my son. "Do your research, Jimmy? I have to go pick up my other children from daycare!" I exclaimed.

Typically, I would use this moment as a time of advocacy, but I was mentally and emotionally exhausted. Navigating judgment and misunderstanding from others can be one of the most emotionally challenging aspects of raising a child on the autism spectrum. It often arises from a lack of awareness or misconceptions about autism, leading to uninformed opinions, hurtful comments, or stares during public meltdowns. Here are some practical approaches and perspectives to help families navigate these situations:

Education as a Tool for Understanding:
Educating those around you is one of the most powerful ways to address judgment.
— Share Information: When friends, family, or acquaintances make assumptions, use it as an opportunity to explain autism in simple, relatable terms. For example, "Autism affects how my child processes the world—loud noises or unexpected changes can feel overwhelming to him."
— Provide Resources: Share articles, videos, or books that explain autism. Sometimes, people need guidance to build understanding.
— Advocate Calmly: If someone is quick to judge, try responding with patience and facts. For instance, "He's not being

difficult; he's communicating his discomfort in the best way he knows how."

Developing Thick Skin and Inner Resilience:
It's hard not to take judgment personally, but building emotional resilience can help protect your peace.
- Focus on Your Child: Remember that your child's well-being matters more than anyone's opinion. You know your child better than anyone else.
- Let Go of Control: You cannot control how others think, but you *can* control how you respond. Shifting your focus inward helps remove the power from judgmental comments or stares.
- Adopt Mantras: Simple reminders, such as "Their judgment is not my reality" or "I'm doing my best, and that's enough," can reinforce your self-confidence during challenging moments.

Choosing Your Circle Wisely:
Surround yourself with people who lift you and understand your journey.
- Find Supportive Communities: Autism support groups, both in-person and online, can be a safe space to share experiences and frustrations without fear of judgment.
- Build Awareness Within Your Family and Friends: Gently set boundaries with unsupportive individuals. For example, "I'd appreciate it if you could listen and try to understand rather than criticize."
- Lean on Allies: Friends, family, or even teachers who "get it" can help you feel less isolated and advocate for your child when others don't.

Preparing for Public Situations:
Handling judgment in public requires a mix of preparation and self-assurance.

- Plan Ahead: If your child struggles with sensory overload or transitions, plan for those triggers by bringing tools like headphones, fidget toys, or visual schedules.
- Ignore the Stares: It's easier said than done, but sometimes, ignoring unhelpful people and focusing on calming your child is the best response.
- Quick Explanations: Some parents find comfort in using brief phrases to diffuse tension. For example: "She has autism, and this is how she copes when overwhelmed.""Thank you for your patience—he's learning to manage this situation." These responses can disarm judgment and often elicit empathy rather than frustration.

Turning Misunderstanding into Advocacy:
Every moment of misunderstanding can become an opportunity for advocacy.

- Model Empathy and Compassion: Responding kindly to those who don't understand can shift their perspective. For example, "I know it might look unusual, but this is how he experiences the world."
- Engage the Curious: If someone genuinely asks questions about autism, answer them. Even small conversations can help dismantle misconceptions.

Protecting Your Mental Health:
The judgment of others can wear you down over time, so prioritizing self-care is essential.

- Connect With Others: Talking with other autism parents can be therapeutic, as they understand the emotional weight of navigating judgment.
- Therapy for Parents: Seeking counseling or therapy can help process feelings of frustration, shame, or anger that arise from others' ignorance.

 — Celebrate Small Wins: Focus on your child's progress, however small, and take pride in your efforts as a parent.

Unfortunately, judgment and misunderstanding are part of the autism journey, but they do not define you or your child. By choosing how you respond, setting boundaries, and surrounding yourself with understanding allies, you can protect your family's peace and advocate for greater awareness. Remember: *You are not alone, and your efforts make a difference.*

After ending the conversation, Messiah and I took our ice cream to go. As I drove home, it made me think about all the times I have had a heated conversation with his father, family members, and even friends regarding the link between autism and vaccines. It is challenging when your views, beliefs, and opinions differ from those of family and friends. In the beginning stage of becoming a mother with a child on the autism spectrum, I used to argue about the correlation between vaccines and autism. Unless I have researched independently or read research from multiple sources, I do not believe half of what I see or hear. Initially, I was convinced that vaccines caused autism until one of my children did not get the "so-called" vaccine (between 12-24 months) that causes it, and he somehow still displayed early signs of autism.

The belief that vaccines cause autism has been a persistent and controversial topic in parenting and autism communities. It's essential to approach this topic with empathy and evidence, as it often stems from fear and a desire for answers rather than malice. Here's how to navigate this sensitive issue:

Acknowledge Their Emotions:
Often, parents who believe vaccines caused their child's autism are often grappling with guilt, confusion, or frustration. They may feel overwhelmed by the lack of clear answers about autism's causes.

- Validate Their Feelings: Statements like, "I understand why you're looking for answers—parenting a child with autism can feel overwhelming," can create an open, respectful dialogue.
- Avoid dismissing their emotions outright, even if you disagree with their conclusion.

Share the Science Respectfully:

Extensive scientific research has found no causal link between vaccines and autism. This theory arose from a discredited study by Andrew Wakefield in 1998, which has since been debunked and retracted. Still, the lingering effects of that misinformation can be powerful.

- Stick to Evidence: Mention key studies, such as those conducted by the CDC, the World Health Organization (WHO), and independent researchers worldwide, which all conclude that vaccines are safe and do not cause autism.
- Explain Correlation vs. Causation: Autism signs often emerge around the same age (12–24 months) as children receive many vaccines. This timing can make it seem like a connection, but correlation doesn't mean causation.
- Highlight the Benefits of Vaccines: Vaccines protect against serious diseases, such as measles and polio, which have life-threatening consequences.

Empathy for Parents Seeking Control:

Believing vaccines cause autism can give parents a sense of control or something tangible to blame, especially when autism's exact causes are complex and not fully understood.

- Frame the Bigger Picture: Autism is believed to result from a combination of genetic and environmental factors. Some research suggests autism begins in utero, long before vaccines are given.

- Share Hopeful Perspectives: Parents should focus on what they can do to support their child in the future, such as therapy, educational tools, and a strong support system.

Boundaries in Conversations:

If someone strongly believes vaccines caused their child's autism and is resistant to other perspectives, it's okay to set boundaries.

- Respectfully Agree to Disagree: Statements like, "I see we have different beliefs on this topic, but I hope we can both focus on supporting our children," can end unproductive arguments.
- Avoid Confrontation. Heated debates rarely change minds. Staying calm and compassionate maintains the relationship, even if you disagree.

Advocacy for Science-Based Awareness:

If you encounter misinformation about vaccines, consider how to advocate for awareness respectfully.

- Share Personal Stories: If you vaccinate your child and feel comfortable sharing your journey, it can help counter fears.
- Connect with Resources: For clear, evidence-based information, recommend organizations like the Autism Science Foundation or the American Academy of Pediatrics.
- Foster Dialogue in Groups: Encourage autism parent groups to host talks with pediatricians or autism experts who can address vaccine concerns in a nonjudgmental way.

To conclude, the belief that vaccines cause autism is rooted in fear, not facts, and responding with compassion rather than judgment can help bridge the gap. Focus on shared goals—assisting children to thrive and supporting one another as parents—rather than getting stuck in divisive debates.

CHAPTER 8

ADVOCATING FOR YOUR CHILD

As time passed, I learned how to advocate in schools, communities, and medical settings. In May 2022, I advocated for Messiah to be transferred to another Dekalb County School District school. I refused to let him be under the guidance of Ms. G. We both needed a change in environment. Sometimes, "the grass is not greener on the other side." As soon as school started, I received phone calls daily regarding Messiah's disruptive behavior. I spent most of this semester (from August to December) going back and forth to his new school because the teachers could not "control him." Instead of genuinely understanding Messiah and using his IEP to create a learning environment suitable for his learning needs, his teacher, Ms. P, made life more complicated than it had to be. She failed to listen to suggestions during parent conferences and IEP meetings.

When I observed her classroom, she mimicked ABA theorists who believed children on the autism spectrum needed to conform to society and act "normal." She acted as if she knew Messiah better than me. Thus, Messiah did not listen to her and disrupted the learning environment often. By January, we created a Behavior Intervention Plan with hopes that his disruptive behavior would decrease so that school personnel, including the speech-language pathologist and occupational therapist, could focus on implementing their interventions to meet his IEP goals. I was so happy when the 2022-2023 school year ended. I requested that he return to his homeschool for Kindergarten.

That year, I began to question if he had other medical issues, such as ADHD/ADD. He struggled with severe impulsivity, attentiveness during instruction, sitting for extended periods, etc. At his yearly appointment with his pediatrician, I shared these concerns, and similar to when I shared my concerns about him possibly having autism, he dismissed them. Instead of conducting an evaluation, he prescribed my son a medication that is used for children and young adults with hallucinations. I was distraught when I got home and read a summary about the medication. At this point, I knew it was time to switch pediatricians.

Becoming a voice for your child in schools, communities, and medical settings is crucial to ensuring they receive the support, understanding, and resources they need to thrive. Advocacy can initially feel daunting, but by educating yourself, building confidence, and fostering partnerships, you can effectively champion your child's needs. Here's how to navigate each setting:

Advocating in Schools:
Ensuring Inclusive Education—Schools play a vital role in a child's development, and advocating for accommodations and support can make all the difference.
–   Learn Your Rights: Familiarize yourself with laws like the Individuals with Disabilities Education Act (IDEA) and Section 504 of the Rehabilitation Act, which guarantees free and appropriate public education (FAPE) and reasonable accommodations.

Individualized Education Plan (IEP) and 504 Plans:
–   Collaborate with teachers and specialists to create a tailored plan.
–   Clearly outline specific needs, such as sensory breaks, communication devices, visual schedules, or one-on-one assistance.

- Document Everything: Keep records of evaluations, IEP meetings, progress reports, and any correspondence with the school. Written communication ensures clarity and accountability.
- Be Proactive, Not Reactive: Attend meetings with specific goals in mind.
- Ask questions like, "What strategies can we implement to help my child succeed?"
- Build Relationships: Treat teachers and administrators as allies. Express gratitude for their efforts while firmly advocating for your child's needs. A collaborative approach can foster a positive, long-term partnership.
- Speak Up for Inclusion: Encourage schools to adopt autism-friendly programs, such as peer support initiatives, sensory spaces, or awareness campaigns, to build students' understanding.

For example, I noticed that Messiah struggled with transitions in class. I advocated for a "first-then" visual schedule, helping him understand what would happen next. This small accommodation significantly improved his focus and participation.

Advocating in the Community: Building Awareness and Acceptance—

Communities shape how children feel about themselves and the world. Advocating for inclusivity can foster understanding and reduce stigma.
- Educate Others: Share your child's experiences to challenge stereotypes and raise awareness about autism.
- Speak to community groups, places of worship, or neighborhood associations about creating inclusive events.
- Push for Accommodations: Encourage businesses, libraries, or recreation centers to make autism-friendly adjustments, such as quiet hours, sensory-friendly spaces, or staff training.

- Participate in Local Initiatives: Join autism organizations, awareness walks, or support groups to amplify your voice and connect with like-minded advocates.
- Model Inclusion: When others see you engaging confidently at playgrounds, stores, or social events, they're more likely to follow suit.

Advocating in Medical Settings: Partnering with Healthcare Providers—

Navigating doctors, therapists, and specialists can be overwhelming, but being an informed and confident advocate ensures your child receives appropriate care.

- Do Your Research: Learn about autism therapies, treatments, and interventions to make informed decisions. Don't be afraid to ask for second opinions.

Prepare for Appointments:

- Write down concerns, observations, and questions ahead of time.
- Share specific examples (e.g., "He becomes overstimulated in noisy environments" or "She's having trouble sleeping through the night").
- Ask Questions: Clarify treatment plans and therapies by asking: "What are the benefits and risks of this intervention?" "How will this help improve my child's specific challenges?"
- Track Progress: Document milestones, challenges, and therapy outcomes using a notebook or app. This information will help you advocate for necessary treatment adjustments.
- Seek Specialists Who Listen: A supportive doctor or therapist will value your input as a parent. Trust your instincts and switch providers if you feel unheard or dismissed.

Finding and Using Your Voice—

Being your child's voice is about persistence, confidence, and courage. Remember: You are the expert on your child.

— Trust Your Instincts: If you sense something isn't right, whether in school, therapy, or the community, don't hesitate to speak up. Your intuition matters.

— Stay Calm and Focused: Under challenging conversations, remain calm and solution-oriented. Focus on facts, your child's needs, and collaboration.

— Seek Support: For guidance, turn to parent support groups, autism organizations, or advocacy groups like the Autism Society or Wrightslaw.

— Celebrate Small Wins: Advocacy takes time, and even small steps forward—like securing one classroom accommodation—are victories worth celebrating.

Advocating for your child requires persistence, collaboration, and courage. By partnering with schools, community members, and medical professionals, you can ensure your child's needs are met and their strengths are celebrated. Remember, every small effort you make contributes to a more inclusive and understanding world for your child and others. I realized no one else would if I didn't advocate for him. I have to be his voice until he learns to use his own.

CHAPTER 9

LEANING ON OTHER PARENTS

After Messiah's diagnosis, I felt completely isolated. Thus, I joined online Facebook support groups (e.g., Autism Mama's Crew, GA Community Autism Support Group, Black Autism Moms (B. A. M), Autism Inclusivity, etc.) where parents shared personal stories, resources, and advice. This helped me tremendously as I began to feel like I belonged. Reading other's stories about challenges they were experiencing with schools, communities, or even their child's behavior was a bit of a relief. I wasn't on this journey alone.

Then, I applied for a parent mentor position in TACA's Mentor Program. TACA: The Autism Community in Action is a nonprofit organization that focuses on improving the outcomes of families and individuals for a better quality of life. After I applied for the mentoring program, TACA officials immediately matched me with a mentor. She had an 18-year-old daughter who was diagnosed with autism at the age of 3 and was currently performing well in school, social, etc., but she only contacted me via email about three times. I did not feel much of a connection with her. Although there was little connection, my mentor said something vital that has remained with me. She told me to stop grieving the past life I imagined for Messiah and embrace our new journey, celebrating our path. That stuck with me, and now I have high hopes for my son as he can achieve the unthinkable.

Connecting with other autism parents can be a lifeline, offering strength, advice, and a sense of solidarity that's hard to find elsewhere. Navigating the journey of raising a child on the autism spectrum often comes with unique challenges, and finding people who "get it" can make all the difference. Here's why building these connections matters and how to foster them:

Shared Understanding and Emotional Support:

One of the most potent aspects of connecting with other autism parents is the immediate understanding and lack of judgment.

– You Don't Have to Explain: Other autism parents understand meltdowns, sensory issues, therapies, and the emotional highs and lows without requiring lengthy explanations.

– Emotional Validation: You'll feel seen and heard when others say, "I've been there too." Knowing you're not alone in your struggles can be incredibly comforting.

– Safe Spaces: Whether online groups or local meetups, autism parent communities are often safe, judgment-free zones where parents can express their fears, frustrations, and joys.

Practical Advice and Resources:

Parents who have walked similar paths can provide sensible advice and tips that professionals may overlook.

– Real-Life Strategies: Other parents can share what worked for them, from managing sensory overload in grocery stores to navigating IEP meetings.

– Recommendations: Parents often exchange referrals for therapists, inclusive schools, doctors, and support services that have made a difference for their child.

– Navigating the System: Experienced parents can offer guidance on accessing early intervention, getting insurance approvals, or understanding special education rights.

Building a Community for Your Child:

Connecting with other parents often creates opportunities for your child to connect with peers with shared experiences.

– Social Opportunities: Organize playdates, sensory-friendly events, or group outings where children feel accepted and supported.

- Peer Role Models: Seeing other kids who communicate or behave differently can help children feel less alone and more understood.

In late 2023, I began creating social groups specifically designed to be sensory-friendly, with flexible rules and understanding participants. Some of our favorite places that hosted sensory-friendly events in the DeKalb County area were Catch Air, Chuck-E-Cheese, High Museum of Art, and the Georgia Aquarium.

Sharing Hope and Celebrating Wins:
In autism parent communities, small victories include a child trying new food, saying a word, or making eye contact.
- Seeing how older children progress or hearing about another parent's success story can inspire and motivate you.
- Encouragement on Tough Days: Other parents can remind you that progress is possible, even if it's not linear.

Learning to Advocate Together:
Parents of children on the autism spectrum often become powerful advocates for their kids. Together, they can amplify their voices and push for meaningful change.
- Advocating in Schools: Collaborate to push for inclusive classrooms, sensory rooms, or teacher training on autism awareness.
- Community Awareness: Partner with other parents to create events like autism awareness walks, library storytimes, or sensory-friendly community activities.
- Policy Change: Parent groups can advocate for better services, funding, and policies at the local or state level.

Reducing Isolation and Building Friendships:
Parenting a child on the autism spectrum can sometimes feel isolating, especially if friends or family don't fully understand. Connecting with other parents fills that gap.

- Building Lasting Friendships: Many parents form deep bonds through shared experiences. These friendships become vital sources of strength.
- Normalizing the Journey: Seeing other families navigating similar challenges helps normalize your experience and reminds you that you're not alone.

In October of 2021, I registered for the Atlanta Walk with the Marcus Autism Center. The purpose of the walk is to build community and raise funds for Autism Speaks, which is an advocacy organization for families and children on the autism spectrum. I created #TeamMessiah, including a few of my friends, his teacher, my grandmother, and his siblings. We had customized shirts, and we looked good as a unit. That event was so much fun, as it was amazing to see so many families present for one purpose. There were so many tee shirt designs, but they uniquely represented each family's fight against autism. It's been a while, but as I write this parent guidebook, I am encouraged to revamp #TeamPayne in 2025 as Messiah, Marjaani, and Micah have all been diagnosed with autism.

Where to Find Other Autism Parents:
If you're unsure where to connect, here are some ideas:
- Local Support Groups: Contact schools, hospitals, or autism organizations for in-person support groups.
- Online Communities: Facebook groups, Reddit forums (like r/autismparents), and parenting blogs offer virtual spaces to connect.
- Events and Workshops: Attend autism awareness events, conferences, or therapy workshops where other families gather.
- Specialized Programs: Many therapy centers or organizations run family-friendly programs or outings where you can meet others.

Connecting with other autism parents creates a circle of support that provides strength, advice, and a shared sense of purpose. Whether you need emotional support, practical strategies, or someone who "gets it," these connections remind you that you're not alone.

As I mentioned before, when I initially received Messiah's autism diagnosis, I felt isolated. I tried to contact a few people I knew had children on the autism spectrum, but I quickly began to realize that they were not my tribe (lack of responses). Thus, I had to find my tribe, which was established in online support groups and communities on Facebook. Have you been able to connect with other autism parents yet? Do you need help looking for ways to find your tribe? Connecting with other autism parents might feel intimidating, but even one small step—like joining an online group or attending a local event—can open the door to meaningful relationships. As you navigate this journey, other parents can become your sounding board, resource hub, and support system. Here is a more defined practical first steps to take today:

Search for a Local Group: Use Google to search for *"autism support groups near me."*

Join an Online Group: Look on Facebook or Reddit for an autism parenting community.

Attend a Local Event: Check with your child's therapy center, school, or local nonprofits for upcoming family-friendly activities.

Reach Out to One Parent: Start small. Talk to another parent at therapy or school and share your story. You'll be surprised at how naturally connections can form.

PART 4

A SPECTRUM OF EMOTIONS

CHAPTER 10

THE HIGHS AND LOWS

Life has a way of humbling you. Becoming an autism parent taught me to embrace moments of joy, laughter, and wonder that remind you of the beauty in your child's world and your journey together. Raising a child on the autism spectrum often comes with unique challenges. Most importantly, it helped me strengthen my faith and reminded me that I needed to always lean on God for understanding. In Hebrews 11, "Now faith is confidence in what we hope for and assurance about what we do not see." When I initially received Messiah's autism diagnosis, my hopes and dreams for his life's successes and future were shattered. However, as time passed, I began to pray for my son and all my children. I stopped having my expectations for God, my children, family, friends, etc. Instead, I started trusting God's plan and believing he would see through all my hopes and desires. Placing expectations on others often leads to disappointment, frustration, and resentment. Trust me, I have experienced enough disappointments to have a healthy expectancy of God and embrace every moment. Embracing every moment, however small or unexpected, can bring hope, connection, and perspective. Here are some ways to embrace every moment:

Finding Joy in Everyday Achievements:
Milestones for children on the spectrum may look different, but they are just as significant, if not more so.
- The Firsts: Whether it's a first word, a first hug, or trying new food, these moments become cherished victories.
- Progress, Not Perfection: Even small steps forward, like making eye contact or saying "hello," are opportunities to celebrate.

For example, when Messiah was younger, he often avoided physical contact. However, one day, I recall him running up to his teacher, Ms. C, at his new school and hugging her. He adored Ms. C and would call her "Mommy." That means a lot for children on the autism spectrum. He associated her with me, a nurturing, caring, strict mom who kept him safe and met his needs.

Laughing at the Unexpected:
Children on the autism spectrum often have unique ways of expressing themselves, leading to funny, heartwarming, or surprising moments.

- Literal Thinking: Their literal interpretations of language can lead to humorous exchanges.
- Unfiltered Honesty: Many children on the autism spectrum speak their minds in ways that bring unexpected laughs.

Wonder Through Their Eyes:
Children on the autism spectrum often experience the world in ways that neurotypical people might not notice.

- Focus on Details: They might point out the beauty in something small, like how light reflects on a puddle or the sound of a bird.
- Passionate Interests: Their deep focus on topics they love—dinosaurs, trains, or numbers—can open doors to shared curiosity and learning.

Connection in Unlikely Places:
Joy often comes from moments of connection, even if they don't resemble typical interactions.

- Shared Laughter: A child's giggle during a favorite game or excitement over a favorite movie can light up the whole room.
- Quiet Bonding: For nonverbal children, smiling, looking, or sitting together in silence can be profoundly meaningful. For example, I learned that Messiah loves music—genres,

including hip hop, R&B, reggae, jazz, etc. Whenever I turned on the music, watching him dance filled our home with joy and made me happy.

Rediscovering Wonder as a Parent:

Parenting a child on the autism spectrum often changes how parents see the world, helping them slow down and appreciate the little things.

— Learning Patience: The journey teaches parents to value progress over perfection and to savor each step forward.

— New Perspectives: Seeing the world through their child's eyes can reignite a sense of wonder and gratitude.

Embracing the Unexpected Path:

Joy comes from realizing that the journey doesn't have to be as meaningful and fulfilling as you imagined.

— Redefining Success: A successful day might make your child feel calm, happy, and understood.

— Celebrating Who They Are: Finding joy in your child's individuality and unique way of engaging with the world brings profound fulfillment.

Sharing the Joy With Others:

Sharing these moments with friends, family, or support groups helps you relive them and inspires others who may be in the same boat.

— Spreading Positivity: Stories of triumphs and funny moments can help shift the narrative about autism to one of celebration.

— Inspiring Others: Parents often encourage one another by sharing the happy milestones they never thought possible.

For example, I often share videos and posts on my social media accounts of Messiah and his siblings having fun and laughing uncontrollably. One outing we had was to the Great Wolf Lodge, an indoor water park in Lagrange, GA. Messiah can be seen sliding down the water slide and laughing uncontrollably as the water splashes on his face and nose. The pure happiness in that moment uplifted my followers.

Parents often say that their children teach them as much as they teach their kids. Finding joy in their child's journey becomes an act of love and resilience. "Amid challenges, there's always light. Our kids show us that happiness isn't in perfection but in those fleeting moments when we laugh, connect, and simply marvel at their unique way of being." Embracing moments of joy, laughter, and wonder doesn't erase the challenges, but it provides the strength and perspective to face them. These moments remind you of the beauty in your child's uniqueness and your family's resilience. How do you embrace moments of joy with your child?

Here are some additional ideas to spark more laughter and joy in your child, tailored to their unique needs and interests. These activities are designed to be playful, sensory-friendly, and adaptable to your child's preferences and comfort level:

Play Silly Games Together:
– Tickle Tag: If your child enjoys physical play, incorporate gentle tickles or silly noises into a game of tag.
– Peekaboo with a Twist: Use a funny hat or toy to "hide" behind for added giggles.
– Copycat Game: Mimic each other's movements, facial expressions, or sounds exaggerated.
– Why it Works: Humor is often found in the unexpected, and kids love seeing parents being playful and goofy.

Embrace Their Unique Sense of Humor:
Every child has their way of finding things funny—lean into what makes *them* laugh.

- If they love funny noises, make silly sound effects, or pretend to sneeze like a cartoon character.
- If they like physical comedy, playfully "trip" or pretend to struggle with something light, like "getting stuck" in a chair.
- Tip: Follow their cues—if they laugh at something, repeat it and build on it.

Sensory-Friendly Fun:

Many sensory activities can be calming and funny for kids on the spectrum.

- Bubble Fun: Try blowing and letting your child pop them, or use a bubble machine for extra excitement.
- Foam Play: Use shaving cream or sensory foam to draw silly faces or make funny shapes on a table.
- Dance Party: Put on their favorite music and dance like no one's watching—use exaggerated moves for extra laughs.
- Why it Works: Sensory play engages their senses while creating opportunities for laughter and joy.

Watch or Create Something Funny:

- Silly Videos: Find videos with animals, slapstick humor, or cartoons that match your child's interests.
- Make Funny Faces: Use a mirror or take silly selfies together.
- Puppet Show: Create voices and personalities for puppets or stuffed animals.

Explore Their Special Interests:

Incorporate their favorite topics or hobbies into playful, lighthearted moments.

- If they love trains, pretend to be a silly conductor or make train noises.
- If they enjoy dinosaurs, act out funny scenarios like a dinosaur that keeps tripping over its tail.

- If they're fascinated by numbers, create a goofy counting game with sound effects or funny voices.
- Why it Works: Kids on the spectrum often light up when their interests are included in playful ways.

Make Everyday Tasks Fun:
Turn routine moments into opportunities for laughter, including:
- Silly Cleanup Races: Pretend to "lose" while your child wins at picking up toys.
- Funny Voices at Mealtime: Use a robot or animal voice while narrating dinner.
- Bath Time Games: Use toys to tell silly stories or let your child "wash" your hands while you make funny reactions.
- Tip: Humor helps transform mundane tasks into bonding opportunities.

Dress-Up and Role Play:
- Silly Costumes: Wear a funny hat or wig and let your child try it.
- Pretend Scenarios: Act out silly roles like a clumsy chef or a superhero who can't stop sneezing.
- Mask Play: Create or wear animal or character masks and pretend to talk or move like them.
- Why it Works: Role-playing encourages creativity and lets kids laugh at lighthearted scenarios.

Enjoy Physical Comedy:
- Pillow Fights: Gentle, playful pillow fights with exaggerated reactions.
- Pretend Falls: Playfully "trip" over a toy or pillow, making it as dramatic as possible.
- Pop-Up Surprises: Peek out from behind furniture or pop into the room unexpectedly with a funny sound.

- Tip: Physical humor can be great for kids who enjoy movement and action.

Create "Oops!" Moments:
- Funny Mistakes: Pretend to "forget" how to do something simple, like putting your shoes on your hands or wearing a hat backward.
- Mix-Up Games: Serve food on a toy plate or mix up the names of toys, letting your child "correct" you.
- Wrong Words: Sing a familiar song but change the words to something silly. For example, "The wheels on the bus go... moo-moo-moo!
- Why it Works: Kids love feeling like they're in on the joke.

Connect Through Nature:
- Outdoor Play: Run through sprinklers, toss leaves in the air, or chase each other with a soft foam ball.
- Nature "Hide and Seek": Pretend to be a silly animal hiding behind trees or bushes.
- Cloud Watching: Lie on your back and make up funny shapes or stories about the clouds.
- Why it Works: Being outdoors can reduce stress and create moments of shared fun and wonder.

Try Interactive Games and Toys Whoopee Cushions:
Classic, harmless fun that gets kids giggling, including:
- Pop-It Games: Play silly challenges with sensory toys like Pop-Its or fidget spinners.
- Interactive Apps: Look for apps with interactive, funny elements, such as talking animals or silly animations. Messiah loves apps in which characters repeat what they say in funny voices or respond to touch with silly reactions.

Involve the Whole Family:
Make laughter a family affair involving siblings, grandparents, or friends.
- Family Comedy Night: Take turns telling silly jokes or doing funny impressions.
- Game Night: Play lighthearted games like Charades, Simon Says, or Twister.
- Group Dance Party: Let everyone enjoy the fun, creating an inclusive and joyful atmosphere.

Laughter is a universal way to connect, and it's even more special when it's sparked by shared moments with your child. The key is to follow their lead, embrace the unexpected, and focus on the joy of being together.

On the other hand, I had to learn how to cope with frustration, exhaustion, and sadness. Having a child on the autism spectrum is frustrating and a profoundly personal journey. There have been plenty of nights I cried myself to sleep due to the effect that this disorder has had on my son and family. I hate that he is nonverbal and unable to express himself. He has come home from school or his father's house with bruises, busted lips, scratches on his face, etc., and the only word he can say is "hurt." Remember, all these emotions are valid and often come with the territory of navigating challenges and uncertainties.

Acknowledging these feelings while finding strategies to care for yourself, manage stress, and maintain resilience is essential. Below are ideas to help you cope during difficult moments:

Acknowledge and Accept Your Feelings:
- Name Your Emotions: Simply saying, "I'm feeling over-whelmed," can be powerful. It allows you to process your emotions rather than suppressing them.

- Remind Yourself It's Okay: Feeling frustrated or sad doesn't make you a bad parent—it makes you human.
- Accept Imperfection: Not every day will go smoothly, and that's okay. It's the effort you put into showing up that matters.

Build a Self-Care Routine:
- Find Small Moments: Even 10–15 minutes alone can recharge you.
- Prioritize Rest: Lack of sleep exacerbates exhaustion. Take turns with a partner or ask someone you trust to help so you can rest.
- Engage in Activities You Love: Reading, meditating, exercising, or listening to music can help you regain energy.
- Tip: Self-care isn't selfish—it's necessary to be the best version of yourself for your child.

Lean on Your Support System
- Family and Friends: Share your feelings with those you trust. Their support can make a difference even if they can't fully understand.
- Parent Support Groups: Connecting with other autism parents can provide solidarity, understanding, and practical advice.
- Therapists or Counselors: Seeking professional guidance can help you process emotions and learn effective coping strategies. Example: Many parents find relief in talking to someone who has "been there" and can reassure them they're not alone.

Practice Stress-Relief Techniques:
- Deep Breathing: A few deep breaths can calm your body and mind in moments of frustration.
- Mindfulness: Focus on the present moment rather than worrying about the future or dwelling on past struggles.
- Journaling: Writing about your feelings can help release pent-up emotions and clarify your thoughts.

- Tip: Apps like Calm or Headspace offer guided meditations and relaxation exercises tailored to busy parents.

Break Challenges into Smaller Steps:
- Focus on What You Can Control: Instead of feeling overwhelmed by everything, identify one small step to address a challenge.
- Celebrate Small Wins: Progress is worth celebrating, no matter how small. This perspective can make challenges feel less daunting.
- Let Go of Perfection: Some days, doing your best is enough. Example: If your child struggles with transitions, focus on making one transition smoother today instead of trying to fix every challenge at once.

Set Boundaries:
- Say No When Needed: You don't have to attend every event or take on every responsibility.
- Protect Your Energy: Limit interactions with people who judge or drain you emotionally.
- Ask for Help: Accept support when offered, whether it's a family member watching your child for an hour or delegating tasks.
- Tip: You don't have to do it all alone—leaning on others is okay.

Reframe Challenges as Opportunities:
- Focus on Strengths: Celebrate what your child can do rather than fixating on what they can't.
- Learn from Setbacks: Each challenge is an opportunity to grow and adapt.
- Embrace Your Role: Remember that you're doing your best to guide your child through their unique journey. Example: A meltdown might feel overwhelming, but it's also a chance to

understand your child's triggers and improve your response next time.

Find Moments of Gratitude and Joy:

—   Reflect on the Good: At the end of the day, write down or think about one joyous moment, no matter how small.
—   Celebrate the Little Things: A smile, a laugh, or a moment of connection can be a powerful reminder of why you keep going.
—   Savor Progress: Remember how far you and your child have come, even if the journey is ongoing.
—   Tip: Gratitude shifts focus from what's going wrong to what's going right.

Educate Yourself and Others:

—   Learn About Autism: Understanding your child's behavior through their lens can reduce frustration and foster empathy.
—   Advocate for Awareness: Helping others understand autism can reduce feelings of isolation and judgment.
—   Set Realistic Expectations. Educating yourself about what's possible can help you approach challenges with clarity and patience. For example, when children struggle with social situations, learning why they find them difficult can lead to tailored solutions rather than frustration.

Focus on Your Long-Term Vision:

—   Remember Your Why: Consider the love and connection that drives you to advocate for your child.
—   Visualize Success: Picture a moment in the future when your hard work pays off, whether it's your child mastering a skill or simply finding happiness in their way.
—   Trust the Journey: Every step, even the hard ones, leads to growth for you and your child.

When You Feel Overwhelmed:
- Take a Timeout: It's okay to step away for a few minutes to gather yourself.
- Ground Yourself: Focus on something physical, like feeling the ground beneath your feet, to anchor yourself in the present.
- Seek Immediate Support: Reach out to someone who can offer empathy or practical help.
- Tip: Stepping away doesn't mean giving up—it means caring for yourself so you can return stronger.

Remember You Are Enough:
- Affirmations: Remind yourself: "I'm doing the best I can, and that's enough."
- Give Yourself Grace: Parenting is hard, and parenting a child with autism comes with extra challenges. Be kind to yourself.
- Reflect on Your Strengths: Think about all you've done for your child and the love that fuels your efforts.

Feeling frustrated, exhausted, or sad is okay—it's part of the process. What matters most is finding ways to care for yourself and recharge so you can continue to show up for your child. Remember, you're not alone, and there's strength in seeking support when needed.

CHAPTER 11

PARENTING WITH RESILIENCE

The topic addressed in this Chapter is probably the most critical strategy to work on, but it is one that I often struggle with as a single parent of multiple children on the autism spectrum. By July of 2023, I had three children diagnosed with autism, either medically or educationally, completed my doctorate program at Walden University in May (Class of 2023, Ed.D in Educational Technology), searching for a virtual job to accommodate every-one's schedule, and was five months pregnant with my last son.

I did not even celebrate my achievements because it is difficult to find reliable support or even hire a babysitter to watch three small children with special needs. Some people offered to have their teenage daughters babysit, but I did not feel comfortable trusting a child with my autistic children. Thus, my self-care and personal maintenance were often neglected.

The demands of raising a child on the autism spectrum can be emotionally, physically, and mentally taxing, making self-care and seeking professional help essential for sustaining both your well-being and your ability to care for your child. Far from being indulgent, these practices are acts of strength that allow you to show up as your best self in challenging moments.

Why does self-care matter?
Self-care is about replenishing your energy so you can meet the demands of parenting with patience and resilience. It's not selfish; it's necessary. Here are examples of why self-care is important:

- Prevents Burnout: Constant stress without relief can lead to emotional exhaustion and overwhelm.
- Models Healthy Behavior: Demonstrating self-care teaches your child the importance of prioritizing their well-being.
- Improves Coping Skills: A well-rested, emotionally balanced parent is better equipped to handle meltdowns, appointments, and advocacy.

For example, during my doctoral journey, I took pride in taking 30 minutes every morning to drink coffee quietly, which helped me feel centered and better prepared to face the day's challenges. I would faithfully wake up at 4:00 AM every morning, drink my coffee, sit quietly for about 10 minutes, and spend about an hour writing my dissertation until it was time to get the kids ready for school. At that time, Messiah had to be dressed and ready to get on his bus by 6:00 AM, and the other children were part-time and did not have to be prepared until about 8:45 AM. Unfortunately, I had to stop drinking coffee during my pregnancy, so I replaced it with a healthy smoothie. Here are some additional self-care strategies:

Small, But Impactful Self-Care Practices:
Physical Care:
- Prioritize sleep, even if it means adjusting routines or asking for help.
- Engage in light exercise like walking, yoga, or stretching to release stress and boost energy.

Mental and Emotional Care:
- Meditate or practice mindfulness, even for a few minutes a day.
- Journal your thoughts to process emotions and gain clarity.
- Listen to uplifting music, podcasts, or audiobooks.

Social Care:
- Schedule regular check-ins with friends or family members who uplift and support you.
- Join local or online parent support groups to connect with others who understand your journey.
- Tip: I realized that self-care doesn't have to be time-consuming; even 5–10 minutes of intentional "me time" can make a difference. I pray that this helps you during your self-care journey.

Seeking Professional Help:

Sometimes, self-care alone isn't enough to navigate the emotional complexities of parenting a child on the autism spectrum. Professional support can provide valuable tools, strategies, and emotional relief. When to consider professional help:
- Persistent Emotional Struggles: If feelings of sadness, anxiety, or frustration linger and impact your daily life.
- Relationship Strain: Parenting stress can affect partnerships or family dynamics. Therapy can help strengthen communication and resolve conflicts.
- Overwhelmed or Burnout: When you feel you can't keep up with the demands or are emotionally depleted.

Types of Professional Support:
Therapists and Counselors:
- Individual Therapy: Helps you process emotions, develop coping mechanisms, and manage stress.
- Family Therapy: Focuses on improving communication and understanding within the family.
- Parent Coaching: Professionals specializing in autism can offer practical strategies tailored to your child's needs.
- Support Groups: Peer-led or therapist-led groups allow parents to share experiences, gain perspective, and feel less isolated.
- Respite Care: Hiring trained caregivers gives you time to rest and recharge while knowing your child is safe.

Overcoming the Stigma of Seeking Help:
- Reframe the Narrative: Seeking help isn't a sign of weakness; it's a proactive step to strengthen yourself and your family.
- Remember the Ripple Effect: When you're supported, your child and family benefit from increased energy and emotional balance.
- Build a Team: Recognize that parenting is a team effort. Including professionals in your support network can lighten the load.

Combining Self-Care and Professional Help:
- Create a Care Plan: Schedule regular self-care practices alongside therapy sessions or coaching.
- Check In With Yourself: Reflect regularly on your emotional state and adjust your support.
- Celebrate Progress: Acknowledge the benefits of self-care and professional help as they strengthen your ability to navigate challenges.

The Long-Term Benefits:
Prioritizing self-care and seeking help builds resilience for the journey ahead.
- Improved Well-Being: Regular self-care reduces stress and enhances overall quality of life.
- Stronger Relationships: Professional help can improve family dynamics and deepen connections with your child.
- Sustained Advocacy: Taking care of yourself ensures you have the energy and focus to advocate effectively for your child's needs.

Taking care of yourself and seeking help when needed is a powerful act of love—for yourself and your child. It's a recognition that you're not just surviving but striving to create a healthy, balanced life for your family. That same month, I sought professional help. The stress from balancing all the children's schedules overwhelmed me. Burnout was evident! This may have been a result of me being pregnant as well, and I was scheduled for my cesarean section in early October.

Yet, I searched for this organization, Therapy for Black Girls, which offers an online space for black girls to encourage mental wellness. Some initiatives included a podcast, a search engine to find therapists, an online support group, and more. I found a therapist, and we began discussing my struggles immediately. Let me share that I have had a few therapists in my lifetime (e.g., struggles with childhood trauma, infertility, and pregnancy loss, relationship strains with my significant other). I am not the woman to shy away from seeking professional help. My therapist not only helped me manage stress but also improved my ability to navigate IEP meetings and medical appointments with confidence.

In August of 2023, I was hired at Georgia Cyber Academy as a Tier 2 Intervention Specialist, and I could not have asked for a better company and department to work for. My stress began to decrease as I did not have to worry about finding help with care for the children before and after school. I could parent effectively and still work to take care of my bills. I enjoyed putting my children on the bus and watching them leave in the afternoon. At work, I built strong relationships with some of my coworkers, and they supported me generously (without any judgment).

Moreover, recognizing your limits and asking for help is one of the most empowering and compassionate things you can do as a parent of children on the autism spectrum. It's an acknowledgment that no one can do it alone and that seeking support is not a sign of failure but of strength and self-awareness. Here are some strategies and perspectives to help you embrace this mindset and take actionable steps:

Understanding the Importance of Recognizing Your Limits:
– Avoiding Burnout: Constantly pushing beyond your limits can lead to exhaustion, resentment, and physical or emotional health issues.
– Modeling Healthy Boundaries: Showing your child that it's okay to ask for help teaches them to do the same when they need support.
– Staying Present means knowing your limits, which allows you to focus on what truly matters instead of spreading yourself too thin. Recognizing your limits doesn't mean you're failing; it means you're prioritizing sustainability for yourself and your family.

Signs It's Time to Ask for Help:
– Physical Symptoms: Fatigue, headaches, or difficulty sleeping may signal stress overload.
– Emotional Strain: Often feeling irritable, hopeless, or overwhelmed.
– Inability to Keep Up: Struggling to balance daily tasks, appointments, and caregiving responsibilities.
– Decreased Patience: Finding it more challenging to respond calmly to your child's needs or behaviors.
– Tip: Pay attention to your body and emotions—these are signals that it's time to delegate or seek support.

Reframing Asking for Help:
– It's a Strength: Recognizing your limits and seeking assistance is a sign of wisdom, not weakness.
– You're Not Alone: Many parents feel the same way, and there's no shame in leaning on others.
– It Benefits Everyone: Getting help ensures you can recharge, which allows you to be more present and patient with your child. For example, I would ask my grandmother to help me babysit as she was retired and has supported me through every

journey of my life, from graduation to the births of my children; she has always been there for me. Unfortunately, she suffered a minor stroke and is still trying to recover mentally and physically from the stroke. Each time she came to my home to babysit, it gave me time to recharge and prepare to handle my children's challenging behaviors with empathy.

Building Your Support Network:
- Family and Friends: Reach out to loved ones willing and able to help, whether babysitting, running errands, or just listening.
- Parent Groups: Join local or online communities of parents raising children on the autism spectrum to share experiences and resources.
- Professionals: Consider hiring respite caregivers, therapists, or counselors for targeted support.
- Educators and School Staff: Partner with teachers and school counselors to ensure your child is supported academically and socially.
- Tip: Be specific about what you need—people are often more willing to help when they understand how to contribute.

How to Ask for Help:
- Be Honest: Share what you're struggling with clearly and vulnerably.
- Be Specific: Instead of saying, "I need help," try, "Could you watch my child for two hours on Saturday?" or "Can you help me with grocery shopping this week?"
- Accept Different Forms of Help: Not everyone can provide hands-on assistance, but emotional support or advice can be equally valuable.
- Express Gratitude: A simple "thank you" goes a long way in maintaining supportive relationships.

Setting Boundaries to Protect Your Energy:
- Learn to Say No: It's okay to decline requests or activities that add unnecessary stress to your life.
- Prioritize Your Time: Focus on what's most essential and let go of less critical tasks or obligations.
- Delegate: Share responsibilities with family members or other caregivers whenever possible.
- Tip: Boundaries aren't about pushing people away—they're about ensuring you can care for what matters most.

Embrace Tools and Resources:
- Autism Organizations: Many organizations offer free or low-cost resources, workshops, and support for families.
- Respite Care: These services provide temporary relief by offering trained caregivers who understand autism.
- Assistive Technology: Tools like communication devices or sensory apps can make everyday tasks more manageable for your child and you.

For example, I found that using an online grocery delivery service, such as Instacart and Kroger Delivery, freed up valuable time to spend with my children. It also relieved me of the stress I would endure if I had to take all of them to the grocery store. There have been times when I had to take them all with me. What was I thinking? Although the experience has its benefits, as they need exposure to social settings, I almost pulled all my hair out: the arguing, eloping, touching everything, etc., was too much for me to handle.

The Benefits of Asking for Help:
- Restored Energy: Time to rest and recharge enables you to return to parenting with renewed focus.
- Emotional Balance: Sharing your struggles lightens the emotional load and reduces feelings of isolation.

- Improved Relationships: When less stressed, you can better connect with your child and loved ones. Reminder: It's not about doing everything alone—creating a village to support you and your child.

What to Do If You Struggle to Ask for Help:
- Start Small: Ask for help with one minor task and build from there.
- Remind Yourself that support is Temporary. It doesn't mean you're giving up control; it's just a temporary lift to help you manage.
- Talk to a Trusted Friend: Sometimes, sharing your reluctance can lead to reassurance and encouragement.
- Consider Therapy: If asking for help feels overwhelming, a counselor can help you explore and overcome these barriers.

Celebrate Your Decision to Seek Help:
- Acknowledge Your Effort: Recognize that asking for help is a proactive step toward creating a healthier life for you and your child.
- Focus on the Benefits: Reflect on how support has improved your mental state, relationships, or ability to meet your child's needs.
- Encourage Others: Share your story with other parents to normalize asking for help and inspire them to do the same. Recognizing your limits and asking for help is one of the most compassionate things you can do for yourself and your child. It ensures you have the strength and resilience to face challenges while creating a support network.

CHAPTER 12

LOVE WITHOUT LIMITS

My journey through autism has been a profoundly transformative experience that reshaped not only how I parent but also how I see the world, myself, and others. It challenges, humbles, and inspires you, often leading to personal growth in unexpected ways. Autism has changed the way I appreciate differences, which I believe is the most beautiful gift of the autism journey. It opened my eyes to the diversity of human experiences and reminded me that there isn't one way to exist or thrive in this world.

Before I became a parent, I was fixated on living life by doing what was always deemed proper and by the "book." I was not performing illegal activities, but I always thought things had to be done a certain way, and I despised change. Today, I have learned to "slow down" and cherish small moments of joy, like my child making eye contact or learning a new word, which they might have overlooked. Each one of my children is unique in their way. Messiah taught me the value of nonverbal communication, including how smiles, touch, and shared moments are a way to express ourselves.

On the other hand, my daughter has been the child who helped me transform my priorities and sense of purpose. I did not talk about her much in this parent guidebook. She was also diagnosed with autism when she was 2 years old. Since her diagnosis, she has taught me the importance of patience and resilience. Marjaani struggles with her emotional regulation and often has meltdowns. But she also started reading when she was 3.5 years old, and we can have mature conversations. Currently, she's excelling in Pre-K. When she returned home from school, we talked daily about school, her friends, her food, classmates who were mean to her, etc. She knows if I am not feeling too good and helps me with her baby brother during those times.

I had to educate myself about autism so that I could appropriately educate others and advocate for my children in IEP meetings, therapies, and even social settings. I transformed from a shy, autism parent to one who confidently advocated for accommodations that helped my children thrive in school. I am happy that all my children thrive in their learning environments today. Messiah is in 1st grade, Marjaani is in Pre-K, and Micah is in PK4.

The beginning of the 2024-2024 school year was challenging for Messiah. His teacher had a difficult time with his behavior, and instead of working together to find a solution, she preferred to send home adverse behavior reports. I refused to allow her to create such a negative narrative about my son when I knew he was dealing with other issues besides autism. I often requested IEP meetings because, by law, if a parent requests an IEP meeting, it has to take place. We met several times to initiate a complete behavioral evaluation, reinstate an old Behavior Intervention Plan, and discuss ways to intrinsically motivate Messiah to exhibit appropriate behavior. The LTSE at his school was phenomenal; she was knowledgeable about ensuring that my son was thriving. He was finally evaluated and diagnosed with ADHD in November 2024.

For the next month, the IEP team saw a tremendous change in his behavior, and I received his first positive phone call. Every day, when he returned home, he showed me his positive behavior report. He would also run off the bus to hug, which was another indicator that he had a good day. How has the autism journey changed you as a parent and person? Below are some ways this journey changes us as parents and individuals.

Learning to See the World Through New Eyes:
- Appreciation for Differences: Autism teaches us to embrace and celebrate neurodiversity. What once seemed unconventional becomes extraordinary.
- Heightened Awareness: We become more attuned to subtle cues, such as how our child expresses joy, discomfort, or connection in unique ways.
- Redefined Milestones: Success is no longer measured by traditional standards but by our child's progress and victories.

Developing Patience and Resilience:
- Patience: The journey requires slowing down, adapting, and meeting our children where they are. This often teaches us to find peace in the process.
- Resilience: Challenges like meltdowns, misunderstandings, or setbacks push us to find strength we didn't know we had.
- Problem-Solving Skills: We become creative and resourceful, learning to navigate obstacles with determination and flexibility. Reminder: Whenever you face a challenge, you build resilience for yourself and your entire family.

Becoming Advocates and Educators:
- Advocacy: Many parents find their voices through advocating for their children's needs in schools, communities, and medical settings.
- Educating Others: We often raise awareness about autism and help others understand and accept our child's uniqueness.
- Confidence in Speaking Up: Over time, we become skilled at asserting what's best for our child, whether in IEP meetings, therapies, or public spaces.

Redefining What It Means to Be a Parent:
- Unconditional Love: The journey teaches us to love without expectations or conditions, simply for who our child is.

- Letting Go of Comparisons: We should stop comparing our parenting or child's progress to others and learn to focus on their unique path.
- Finding Joy in the Present: Autism teaches us to live in the moment, celebrating today's victories instead of worrying about tomorrow's challenges.
- Parenting becomes less about following a predefined path and more about co-creating a journey with our child.

Strengthening Emotional Depth:
- Empathy: We become more empathetic toward our child and others who struggle or are misunderstood.
- Emotional Awareness: The journey often heightens our sensitivity to emotions, both ours and our children's, teaching us to connect on a deeper level.
- Gratitude: Small moments of progress and connection fill us with gratitude in ways that redefine joy.
- I am grateful for my autism journey because I now see beauty in my children's "different" way of interacting with the world. I have also learned to appreciate those differences in others.

Learning to Navigate Judgment and Misunderstanding:
- Thicker Skin: Dealing with stares, unsolicited advice, or misconceptions makes us stronger and more self-assured.
- Reframing Criticism: Instead of letting judgment discourage us, we learn to focus on what truly matters—our child's well-being and happiness.
- Teaching Acceptance: We become examples of compassion, advocating for kindness and understanding toward all. Reminder: These challenges often ignite a deeper passion for building a more inclusive and understanding world.

Building a Deeper Connection with Your Child:
- Learning Their Language: Whether through gestures, devices, or other forms of communication, we become experts in connecting with our children in ways that work for them.
- Celebrating Who They Are: We come to appreciate the quirks and traits that make our children uniquely them.
- Mutual Growth: As we guide and support our children, they teach us patience, creativity, and unconditional love.

Becoming More Purpose-Driven:
- Focus on What Truly Matters: The journey often strips away superficial concerns, allowing us to focus on love, growth, and connection.
- Advocating for Change: Many parents become champions for inclusivity, accessibility, and understanding in their communities.
- Legacy of Compassion: The lessons we learn on this journey shape how we engage with the world and inspire us to improve it for others. The autism journey doesn't just change us as parents—it transforms our priorities and sense of purpose.

Fostering Personal Growth:
- Letting Go of Control: Autism teaches us that we can't control everything, and that's okay. Growth often comes from adapting to the unexpected.
- Reframing Success: We learn to define success by effort, progress, and joy rather than societal expectations.
- Strengthened Identity: The journey shapes us into stronger, more compassionate individuals and often helps us discover hidden strengths. Personal growth isn't always easy, but it's one of the journey's greatest gifts.

Finding a Community:
- Shared Experiences: Connecting with other parents of children on the spectrum fosters a sense of belonging and mutual support.
- Learning from Others: Hearing stories of resilience, creativity, and success from others inspires and motivates us.
- Giving Back: Over time, we often feel called to help others start their journeys, creating a cycle of support and compassion.

The autism journey profoundly changes us. It challenges our assumptions, strengthens our resolve, and opens our hearts to a deep love and understanding we might never have experienced otherwise. While the road can be difficult, it is rich with moments of growth, connection, and purpose that shape us into better parents, partners, and people.

I did not grow up with a parent expressing their love for me. I started recognizing its negative impact on my self-esteem and establishing and retaining positive and healthy relationships in adulthood. When I became a parent, I did not want that negative effect on my children. Thus, I have learned what unconditional love means and how to show it to my children. Reaffirming unconditional love for a child, especially one on the autism spectrum, is a powerful way to nurture their self-esteem, sense of security, and emotional well-being. Here are ways to consistently show and express this love:

Verbal Expressions:
- Say It Often: Tell your child you love them daily, even if they struggle to express their feelings. For example, "I love you just the way you are."
- Praise Effort, Not Just Outcomes: Celebrate their hard work and unique abilities, even in small achievements. Example: "I'm so proud of how hard you worked on that puzzle."

– Acknowledge Their Unique Traits: Help them feel valued for who they are, not just for what they do. For example, "I love how curious you are about the world.

Physical Affection:
– Adapt to Their Comfort Level: Some children on the spectrum may prefer gentle physical contact like a high-five, while others may love hugs.
– Routine Touchpoints: Incorporate moments of connection like holding hands, a bedtime kiss, or sitting close during storytime.

Quality Time Together:
– Follow Their Interests: Engage in their favorite activities, even if it's something you don't fully understand (e.g., learning about their favorite topic or character).
– Create Special Rituals: Develop daily or weekly routines for the two of you, like cooking together, a nighttime story, or a sensory-friendly outing.

Emotional Support:
– Be Their Safe Place: Remind them that it's okay to have hard days and you'll always be there to help. Example: "I know that noise was overwhelming, but you're safe with me."
– Be Patient and Understanding: Show empathy during meltdowns or challenging behaviors by remaining calm and supportive.

Actions that Speak Volumes:
– Advocate for Them: Whether in school, medical settings, or social situations, being their voice shows you're on their side no matter what.
– Celebrate Their Individuality: Show them you value their uniqueness by embracing their quirks and special interests.

- Apologize and Repair: If you lose your temper or make a mistake, model unconditional love by apologizing and reassuring them.

Reassure Through Tough Times:
- Use Visual and Verbal Cues: To remind nonverbal children you care, you can use picture cards, gestures, or a calm tone of voice.
- Highlight Your Bond: Use phrases like: "You're my favorite person to spend time with." "No matter what happens, I'll always love you."

By consistently expressing unconditional love, your child will grow up knowing they are valued and supported for who they are. This foundation fosters confidence, emotional resilience, and a sense of belonging that will carry them through life.

PART 5

LOOKING TOWARD THE FUTURE

CHAPTER 13

SUPPORTING THEIR INDEPENDENCE

Fostering life skills and confidence for children and young adults on the autism spectrum is essential for helping them achieve independence and navigate the following stages of life, whether it's school transitions, employment, or daily living. The biggest challenge I experienced with Messiah and all my children was building life skills, such as self-care and routines (e.g., brushing their teeth, dressing themselves, and toileting). By January of 2022, I bought three children pull-ups and wipes. Can you imagine how much money I was spending on this?

Luckily, in August of 2022, I found a company, S2 Medical Supply, that provided free supplies like pull-ups and bed pads for children with disabilities. S2 Medical Supply is a reputable provider of medical supplies specializing in solutions for children and adults. Their product offerings include incontinence supplies, catheters, and ostomy products. They accept Medicaid, Medicare, and private insurance, ensuring accessibility for many customers. Messiah received free pull-ups and pads for a year, funded through Medicaid. Once his Medicaid ended, expenses for these essential items came out of my pocket.

After Malakai was born in October 2023, I bought diapers, pull-ups, and wipes for four children. Honestly, this was impacting me financially, emotionally, and mentally. The following year, I went cold turkey with all the children and made them wear underwear. I started with Messiah, who was now in the 1st grade.

His new teacher helped help me potty train him. When he got dressed in the morning, I let him use the restroom, and then, as he got dressed, we transitioned from pull-ups to his favorite Super Mario Bros. underwear. It helped them buy their favorite character underwear during potty training. I also used visual cards, pottery training seats, and a reward system during this process. At school, his teacher, Ms. R., allowed him to go to the restroom every hour. By September 2024, he was fully potty trained.

That same month, I started the same process with Marjaani. With the help of her Pre-K teachers, she was fully potty trained by the end of the month. I had also purchased her favorite character panties, Frozen, and I watched in amazement as she excitedly picked out her favorite pair of panties to wear daily. Finally, I potty trained Micah, and he was already ready because he had been watching his siblings for the last few months. He requested Spiderman underwear, and he started the transition during Thanksgiving break. By December of 2024, my little ones were fully potty trained.

Because they are still reasonably young, I have been celebrating this moment with them. They occasionally have accidents but know how to clean themselves up and change into a clean pair of undies. I am still building a bath routine, but they all know how to brush their teeth and dress independently (while I monitor). I typically break tasks into small steps. We've also been working on household responsibilities, such as cleaning their rooms, making their beds, and cleaning the table after breakfast, lunch, and dinner. What challenges do you experience with your child in building life skills? Here are strategies and resources to support this journey:

Building Life Skills:
Self-Care Skills:
- Teach routines like brushing teeth, grooming, bathing, and dressing.
- Break tasks into small steps using visuals, schedules, or checklists.

Communication Skills:
- Encourage verbal, non-verbal, or alternative communication (e.g., PECS or AAC devices).
- Practice everyday conversations like asking for help or ordering at a restaurant.

Time Management:
- Use timers, calendars, or visual schedules to teach the concept of time and how to manage it.
- Start with small, achievable goals like completing a 5-minute task.

Money Management:
- Practice identifying coins and bills, using a calculator, and counting change.
- Role-play situations like grocery shopping or managing a small allowance.

Household Responsibilities:
- Teach simple chores like making the bed, folding clothes, or setting the table.
- Use checklists or apps to create a sense of routine and accomplishment.

Transportation Skills:
- Introduce concepts like reading maps, planning routes, and using public transportation.
- Start with small, supervised trips to build confidence.

Fostering Confidence:

Set Achievable Goals:
- Break tasks into small steps and celebrate progress, not just outcomes.
- Focus on strengths to build self-esteem and encourage a sense of achievement.

Encourage Decision-Making:
- Allow choices in daily activities to develop decision-making skills.
- Use "either-or" options initially to avoid overwhelming them.

Build Social Skills:
- Practice social interactions in low-pressure settings, such as playgroups or small gatherings.
- Use role-playing to rehearse real-life scenarios like greetings, introductions, or problem-solving.

Highlight Strengths and Interests:
- Encourage activities that align with your child's passions, such as art, technology, or music.
- Celebrate unique talents and provide opportunities to showcase them.

Model Self-Advocacy:
- Teach your child to express their needs and preferences confidently.
- Encourage them to ask for accommodations at school, work, or community.

Preparing for the Next Stages of Life:

Transitioning to Adulthood:
- Introduce vocational or technical skills during teenage years through internships, volunteer work, or part-time jobs.

- Explore post-secondary education options, trade schools, or autism-friendly programs.

Focus on Emotional Regulation:
- Teach coping strategies for stress, like deep breathing, sensory tools, or mindfulness techniques.
- Provide scripts or visual aids for navigating difficult emotions.

Independent Living Skills:
- Practice basic cooking, budgeting, and household management in real-life contexts.
- Start with supervised tasks and gradually increase independence.

Explore Employment Opportunities:
- Identify strengths that can translate into jobs (e.g., attention to detail for data entry).
- Connect with organizations like The Arc or Autism Speaks Workplace Inclusion Programs.

Encourage Peer Support:
- Join autism support groups where they can meet peers with similar experiences.
- Foster friendships through shared interests and structured social activities.

Helpful Resources:
Apps for Life Skills:
- Choice works: Visual schedules and decision-making support.
- Todo Math: Basic math skills for money management.
- Money Up!: Teaches money and shopping skills.

Books:
- "Life Skills Activities for Secondary Students with Special Needs" by Darlene Mannix.

- "Preparing for Life: The Complete Guide for Transitioning to Adulthood for Those with Autism" by Dr. Jed Baker.

Programs and Organizations:
- Project SEARCH: Employment training for young adults with disabilities.
- Easterseals Life Skills Programs: Focus on employment and independent living.
- Autism Society Transition Toolkits: Resources for planning life transitions.

Teaching a child on the autism spectrum to self-advocate is a critical life skill that builds confidence, fosters independence, and helps them communicate their needs. Here's how to approach it in age-appropriate ways:

Early Childhood (Ages 3–7):

Recognize Feelings:
- Teach your child to identify and name their emotions using visual aids or emotion cards. Example: "When you feel frustrated, you can tell me, 'I need help.'"

Make Choices:
- Offer simple choices to give them a sense of control. Example: "Do you want to play with blocks or draw?"

Use Visual Tools:
- Use communication boards or apps to help non-verbal children express their needs.

Model Asking for Help:
- Demonstrate phrases like, "Can you help me?" or "I need a break."
- Practice these during low-stress situations.

Middle Childhood (Ages 8–12):

Teach "I Statements":
- Introduce simple scripts: "I feel _____ because _____. I need _____." Example: "I feel overwhelmed because it's loud. I need some quiet time."

Practice Speaking Up in Safe Spaces:
- Role-play scenarios like asking a teacher for help or telling a friend about a sensory preference.

Encourage Self-Awareness:
- Help them identify triggers and preferences. Example: "Do bright lights bother you? You can say, 'Can we turn the lights down?'"

Introduce Accommodations:
- Help them understand the tools or accommodations they use, like noise-canceling headphones or fidget toys, and how to explain their purpose.

Teen Years (Ages 13–18):

Involve Them in IEP/504 Meetings:
- Encourage them to participate and express their goals or needs. Example: "I learn best when instructions are written down."

Teach Advocacy for Social Boundaries:
- Help them communicate when they need personal space or don't want to engage in certain activities. For example, "I don't like hugs, but I'm happy to give a high five."

Practice Real-Life Scenarios:
- Role-play situations like ordering food, asking for a sensory-friendly space, or explaining their needs to others.

Explore Self-Advocacy in Work or Volunteering:
– Teach them to communicate their needs in professional settings. Example: "I work better in quiet environments.

Young Adulthood (18+):
Encourage Self-Reflection:
– Help them articulate their strengths, challenges, and accommodations needs. For example, "What helps you feel calm when stressed?"

Prepare for Transition Planning:
– Teach them to advocate for themselves in post-secondary education, employment, or independent living.

Introduce Legal Rights:
– Help them understand laws like the Americans with Disabilities Act (ADA) and their rights in education, work, and public spaces.

General Strategies for All Ages:
Celebrate Their Efforts:
– Acknowledge every attempt at self-advocacy to build their confidence.

Create Safe Practice Environments:
– Allow them to practice speaking up in familiar and supportive settings.

Foster Self-Confidence:
– Reinforce their value and remind them that their needs and preferences matter.

Collaborate with Educators and Therapists:
- Work with professionals to teach and reinforce advocacy skills across settings.

Equipping your child with the tools to self-advocate empowers them to navigate their world confidently and independently.

CHAPTER 14

DREAMING BIG, ADJUSTING WISELY

Reframing success and happiness for a child on the autism spectrum often means moving away from traditional or societal definitions and embracing a personalized perspective. It's about celebrating progress, honoring individuality, and finding joy in meaningful moments. For Christmas in 2024, I celebrated my children by creating a new tradition that the kids enjoyed. Now that they are older, they recognize the small joys of our life, being a part of our family. Five days before Christmas, I planned and prepared fun activities for them. I also know that they get overstimulated, so I planned wisely. Some of the activities included a Grinch Movie Night. I cooked nachos and cheese, had popcorn with M&M's, Nerds gushers, and Grinch punch (yes, it was green). We also wore matching Christmas pajamas and took pictures of our trees. The smiles on their faces let me know that they were having a fantastic time.

Towards the middle of the movie, I let them choose one gift from under the tree to open. I must admit, I am mastering this mommy role. Marjaani was the first to open her gift. As she quickly tore the paper off the gift, she began to see she had a Mini BarbieLand PLayhouse. She immediately jumped up and told me, "Thank you, Mommy! I love it!" Micah had a Play-Doh set, and Messiah received a Spiderman glove and an artificial web shooter. I helped them all assemble their new toys and sat back and watched them laugh and play with their new toy. When I buy gifts for my children, I strategically try to include their unique talents, passions, interests, and abilities. That night, they tucked me into bed by 10 PM. Motherhood is exhausting, but it is the best gift from God.

Here are some strategies and insights to help parents reframe these concepts:

Defining Success Differently:
Focus on Progress, Not Perfection:
- Celebrate small victories and milestones, no matter how minor they may seem to others. For example, learning to tie shoes, trying new food, or making eye contact is worth celebrating.

Highlight Their Strengths:
- Recognize your child's unique talents, passions, and abilities, whether they involve music, art, or a love for details.
- Success doesn't have to conform to societal norms—it can be as simple as finding joy in one's unique interests.

Set Individualized Goals:
- Base goals on your child's needs and capabilities, not on comparisons to peers. For example, success might mean learning to communicate with a picture board or mastering a daily living skill.

Redefine Independence:
- Independence can look different for every child. It might mean learning to self-advocate, participating in group activities, or navigating parts of the day with minimal support.

Reframing Happiness:
Find Joy in the Present:
- Focus on what makes your child happy now, whether spinning in circles, watching their favorite show, or spending time with family.
- Recognize that their happiness may look different from yours but is just as valuable.

Value Their Unique Experiences:
- Accept that your child's version of happiness might not align with neurotypical expectations—and that's okay. For example, a quiet day organizing toys might bring your child more joy than a loud birthday party.

Teach Self-Acceptance:
- Help your child embrace their identity by modeling pride and accepting who they are.

Appreciate Moments of Connection:
- Happiness might come from shared experiences, such as a hug, a smile, or laughter at a funny moment. These are the building blocks of a fulfilling life.

Strategies for Parents:
Let Go of Comparisons:
- Avoid measuring your child against societal benchmarks or other children. Your child's path is unique.

Celebrate Diversity:
- Embrace the idea that difference is not less. Teach your child that their individuality is a strength, not a limitation.

Reframe Setbacks:
- View challenges as opportunities for growth and learning for your child and yourself.

Emphasize Emotional Well-Being:
- Prioritize your child's mental and emotional health over academic, social, or other external measures of success.

Before my children started Winter Break, I contacted their teachers regarding their social and emotional learning. It is easy to overlook this development because we want our children to succeed academically. Each development is simultaneously essential. On Friday, December 13, 2024, I received a call from Marjaani's Pre-K teacher, sharing that Marjaani was being uncooperative in the classroom. It only took for her to hear my voice to calm down. By noon, her teachers shared that she had a good rest of the day. When she returned home, I rewarded her with Oreos and milk. Since she loves Oreos and milk, I used this as an incentive to celebrate her daily wins.

Marjaani often has good school days, but her social-emotional learning needs are not met in her classroom. I contacted all the children's teachers and inquired about social-emotional learning programs at their schools. To date, I have not received a solid response. Thus, I will have to conduct my research and get my children what they need. I miss our former OT because she focused heavily on their SEL. Here are some practical ideas to celebrate success and foster happiness:

Create a "Success Journal":
– Keep a log of accomplishments, big or small, to remind you and your child how far they've come.

Incorporate Their Passions:
– Build their strengths into daily routines. If they love puzzles, use them as a reward or as part of learning activities.

Celebrate Their Way:
– Tailor celebrations to your child's preferences. If loud parties overwhelm them, celebrate milestones with a quiet family dinner or an activity they enjoy.

Involve Them in Defining Goals:
– As they grow, let them have a say in what success looks like for them.

Mindset Shift for Parents:

See the World Through Their Eyes:
— Shift your perspective to understand what success and happiness look like for your child.

Remember, it's Their Journey:
— Success isn't about achieving societal benchmarks—it's about your child living a fulfilling life on their terms.

Celebrate the Journey, Not Just the Destination:
— Appreciate every step, including the challenges, as they shape your child's unique story. By reframing success and happiness, you create a foundation where your children can thrive, be themselves, and feel valued for who they are.

On the other hand, I have started to consider long-term care and financial planning for my children. Creating a roadmap for long-term care and financial planning for a child on the autism spectrum is essential to ensure their well-being and security as they grow into adulthood. It involves proactive planning, leveraging available resources, and building a support network. Here's how to get started:

Step 1: Assess Current and Future Needs:
Evaluate Care Needs:
— Consider the type of support your child may require now and in the future: medical, educational, daily living skills, and employment opportunities. Examples: Will they need housing, transportation, or job training assistance as they become adults?

Understand Long-Term Goals:
- Discuss goals such as independent living, vocational training, or college.
- Create realistic expectations based on your child's abilities and interests.

Step 2: Establish Financial Security:
Set Up a Special Needs Trust (SNT):
- You can protect your child's eligibility for government benefits (such as SSI and Medicaid) while setting aside funds for their future.
- Funds in the trust can be used for things like housing, therapy, and education.

Open an ABLE Account:
- Tax-advantaged savings accounts specifically for individuals with disabilities.
- These accounts allow for saving without jeopardizing government benefits.

Create a Budget:
- Estimate future expenses, including therapies, medical care, housing, and recreational activities.
- Factor in inflation and unexpected costs.

Consider Life Insurance:
- A policy with your child as the beneficiary can provide financial support if you can no longer care for them.

Step 3: Plan for Legal and Financial Protection:
Establish Guardianship or Power of Attorney:
- Depending on your child's abilities, you may need to explore guardianship or a power of attorney when they turn 18.

- Alternatives like supported decision-making can empower your child while providing guidance.

Draft a Letter of Intent:
- Outline your child's needs, preferences, daily routines, medical history, and future goals.
- This document can guide caregivers or family members if you cannot care for your child.

Work with a Financial Advisor:
- Consult a professional experienced in special needs planning to optimize your savings and investment strategies.

Step 4: Explore Government and Community Resources:
Apply for Benefits:
- Your child may qualify for Research Supplemental Security Income (SSI), Medicaid waivers, and other programs.

Access Community Support:
- Join local autism organizations for housing, vocational training, and respite care resources. The Arc, for example, offers programs to help families with long-term care planning.

Leverage School Transition Programs:
- Work with your child's school to develop a transition plan through their IEP, focusing on life skills, employment, and post-secondary education.

Step 5: Plan for Housing and Independent Living:
Explore Housing Options:
- Options include group homes, assisted living, supported independent living, or living with family.
- Discuss and research housing opportunities early, as waitlists can be extended.

Teach Independent Living Skills:
- Begin teaching fundamental skills like cooking, cleaning, and managing money early.
- Use visual aids, checklists, or apps to support learning.

Step 6: Build a Circle of Support:
Identify Trusted Individuals:
- Create a network of family members, friends, and professionals who can step in if needed.
- Ensure they understand your child's needs and preferences.

Engage Siblings or Relatives:
- Have honest conversations with siblings or relatives about their potential future role in your child's care.

Find Professional Resources:
- Work with therapists, case managers, and financial planners to ensure a comprehensive support system.

Step 7: Update Plans Regularly:
Review and Adjust Annually:
- Reassess your financial, legal, and caregiving plans to reflect your child's changing needs and circumstances.

Stay Informed:
- Keep up with changes in disability laws, benefits, and resources to ensure you're maximizing opportunities.

Plan for Your Future:
- Ensure your retirement and estate planning align with your child's long-term needs.

Key Resources to Get Started:

Special Needs Trusts:
–   Work with an attorney specializing in disability law to create a trust.

ABLE Accounts:
–   Visit www.ablenrc.org for guidance on opening and managing an ABLE account.

The Arc's Center for Future Planning:
–   Offers tools and support for long-term planning: www.thearc.org.

Parent Support Groups:
–   Connect with other families to share experiences and learn about additional resources.

CHAPTER 15

EMBRACING THE SPECTRUM OF LOVE

I have come to the end of my parent guidebook, and I am saddened as there is so much more information to share. But I don't want this guidebook to be an overwhelming textbook you must read in college. I have a doctorate, so trust me when I say that I understand how the words on a page can be attacking. Also, I am not a trained autism professional; this guidebook is based on my personal experiences with my children on the autism spectrum.

However, I hope I was able to provide some clear and concise tools and strategies that can help you as you navigate your journey through autism. Remember that each of us has been uniquely designed, and our journey will look and sound different. Please accommodate your child and family according to your individual needs. Use this time to reflect on your journey. I've included some reflection points at the end of each section for you to proactively think about and start planning for your journey, whether your child is newly diagnosed or you've been navigating this journey for a while and feel hopeless. It's never too late to reframe success for your child.

In this final Chapter, I reflect on the transformative power of love and acceptance and describe how I have found beauty in the challenges and uniqueness of autism. Reflecting on these values reveals how they shape your child's life and your journey as a parent. Love and acceptance are more than emotional responses—guiding principles that redefine how you approach challenges, celebrate milestones, and build relationships. Here's a reflection on their profound impact:

How Love Transforms:

Focus on Connection Over Perfection:
— Love reminds you to cherish your unique bond with your child. It helps you see beyond societal expectations and focus on what truly matters: their happiness, growth, and sense of belonging.

Fuel for Resilience:
— Love carries you through moments of frustration, exhaustion, or uncertainty. It helps you persevere when navigating obstacles and fiercely advocate for your child's needs.

Joy in Everyday Moments:
— It teaches you to find beauty in small victories—a shared laugh, a breakthrough in communication, or your child's pure joy in their favorite activity.

The Role of Acceptance:

Embracing Differences:
— Acceptance shifts your perspective from "fixing" to "celebrating." It allows you to honor your child's individuality and recognize that their differences are strengths, not limitations.

Breaking Free of Comparisons:
— When you accept your child for who they are, you let go of comparisons to neurotypical peers. This frees both you and your child from unrealistic expectations and fosters self-confidence.

Creating a Safe Space:
- Acceptance fosters an environment where your child feels loved unconditionally. This security empowers them to explore, grow, and express themselves authentically.

The Impact on You as a Parent:
Personal Growth:
- Loving and accepting your child transforms you. It challenges you to be more patient, empathetic, and open-minded. It broadens your understanding of the world and deepens your capacity for compassion.

Strength in Vulnerability:
- Acceptance requires courage. It involves acknowledging fears and uncertainties while moving forward with hope and love. This vulnerability makes one stronger and more connected to one's child.

Redefining Success:
- You learn that success isn't about fitting into predefined molds but about your child feeling valued, supported, and happy.

The Ripple Effect of Love and Acceptance:
Empowering Your Child:
- When your child knows they are loved and accepted, they gain the confidence to advocate for themselves, explore their interests, and embrace their identity.

Inspiring Others:
- Your journey can inspire family, friends, and the community to approach autism with greater understanding and kindness.

Building a Legacy of Inclusion:
- Love and acceptance extend beyond your family, creating a more inclusive society where all differences are celebrated.

Take a moment to reflect on how your love and acceptance have shaped your child's life and your own. What moments stand out as examples of how these values have guided you? What have you learned from your child about the meaning of love and acceptance? By choosing love and acceptance, you create a foundation for your child to thrive and flourish, transforming their world and your own. Finally, finding beauty in the challenges and uniqueness of autism is about shifting perspective to recognize the extraordinary within the ordinary. While the journey can be demanding, it is filled with profound, meaningful, and uniquely beautiful moments. Here's how to embrace and celebrate the experience:

The Beauty of Unfiltered Expression:
- Children on the autism spectrum often express themselves in raw and genuine ways. Their emotions, joys, and passions are not filtered by societal expectations, creating moments of pure authenticity. For example, watching your child light up when engaging in a favorite activity or hearing them uniquely share their thoughts can be profoundly moving.

Unique Perspectives on the World:
- Children with autism often see the world through a lens that reveals details and patterns others might overlook.
- Beauty in focus: A deep fascination with a specific subject, such as trains, numbers, or nature, highlights a focused and passionate mind. For example, observing your child's joy in organizing items or excitement over a unique interest reminds you to appreciate the beauty in details.

Creativity and Innovation:
- Individuals on the autism spectrum often think in ways that challenge conventional ideas, offering fresh perspectives and creative problem-solving. For example, a child who finds imaginative ways to communicate or play demonstrates creativity and thrives outside typical boundaries.

Resilience Through Challenges:
- Facing and overcoming challenges strengthens your child and your entire family. Each hurdle surmounted is a testament to resilience, perseverance, and unconditional love. For example, celebrating a milestone, like learning a new skill or expressing a need, is an accomplishment that brings immense pride and joy.

Honoring Individuality:
- The differences that come with autism are reminders of the beauty in diversity. Every individual contributes something unique and valuable to the world. For example, a child who thrives in their routine or communicates specially teaches those around them the importance of patience and acceptance.

Deepening Family Bond:
- Navigating the autism journey together strengthens family connections. Each family member learns to adapt, support, and celebrate one another's roles and efforts. For example, the shared joy of a family outing that accommodates everyone's needs can bring a deeper sense of togetherness.

Finding Joy in the Unexpected:
- While autism brings challenges, it also introduces unexpected delight—moments that might not happen in a more typical journey. For example, the first time your child expresses

affection uniquely or surprises you with a skill they've mastered is a moment of profound beauty.

Redefining Success and Happiness:
- Autism teaches parents to value progress over perfection and redefine happiness. It's not about fitting into molds but about thriving as an individual. For example, watching your child achieve a goal that aligns with their abilities rather than external standards can be more rewarding than traditional measures of success.

How to Embrace the Beauty in Autism:
Document the Moments:
- Keep a journal or photo album to capture and reflect on growth, joy, and love moments.

Celebrate Small Victories:
- No milestone is too small to celebrate; every achievement is meaningful.

Learn from Your Child:
- Let their perspective teach you about patience, creativity, and joy in the present moment.

Surround Yourself with Support:
- Connect with others on the same journey to share experiences and see the beauty they've found.

Practice Gratitude:
- Focus on what makes your child unique and appreciate the lessons they teach you daily.

While parenting a child with autism comes with challenges, it is also one of extraordinary beauty. It invites you to see the world differently, celebrate individuality, and redefine what love, success, and joy look like. Each day, your child's uniqueness teaches you to slow down, cherish the small things, and find beauty in the unexpected.

A LETTER TO MY CHILDREN

Dear Messiah, Marjaani, Micah, & Malakai,

As I write this, my heart is full of love, gratitude, and admiration for each of you. I want you to know how profoundly you've shaped my life and how thankful I am for the privilege of being your parent. I knew my life would never be the same from the moment I held you. What I didn't realize was how much *you* would teach *me*. In your unique ways, you've shown me the beauty of patience, the power of resilience, and the joy of seeing the world through a different lens.

You've taught me what it truly means to love.
Your love is pure and unconditional. It has taught me to let go of expectations and embrace the present moment. You've shown me that love is not about perfection but about being there, understanding, and celebrating the little things that make us who we are.

You've taught me to slow down and notice the details.
In your own ways, you've helped me see the magic in things I might have overlooked: the patterns in the leaves, the melody in a favorite song played over and over, or the joy in a perfectly organized row of toys. You've shown me that beauty exists all around us if we just take the time to look.

You've taught me resilience.
I've watched you face challenges with courage and determination, inspiring me to do the same. You've shown me that progress isn't

about comparing ourselves to others but celebrating how far we've come, one step at a time.

You've taught me to celebrate differences.
Your uniqueness is your strength, and it has opened my eyes to a world filled with diversity and beauty. You've taught me that differences make life richer and that embracing them leads to deeper understanding and love.

You've taught me to laugh and find joy in unexpected places.
Your laughter is one of the most beautiful sounds in the world. Even on the hardest days, your giggles and smiles remind me that there's always room for joy, even amid challenges.

You've taught me to be brave.
Your courage—whether it's trying something new, speaking up for yourself, or simply navigating a world that doesn't always understand you—has inspired me to be braver, too.

Most of all, you've taught me to be a better version of myself.

Being your parent has pushed me to grow in ways I never thought possible. You've taught me patience when I felt I had none, empathy when I didn't understand, and strength when I felt weak.

Thank you for being exactly who you are. Thank you for teaching me lessons no book or class could. Thank you for filling my life with a profound love that words never truly capture. I am so proud of you—not just for what you accomplished but for who you are. You are my greatest teacher, my greatest joy, and my greatest blessing.

With all my love,
Mommy

FINAL WORDS OF ENCOURAGEMENT AND SOLIDARITY FOR OTHER PARENTS

To All Fellow Parents on This Journey,

I see you. I see your strength, resilience, tears, and endless love. You are not alone in this. Parenting a child on the autism spectrum is not an easy road, but it is a profoundly meaningful one. It will stretch you in ways you never imagined, challenge you to the core, and yet—fill your heart with a love so fierce and unconditional that it defies words.

There will be days when the weight feels too heavy, and you doubt yourself or wonder if you're doing enough. On those days, please remember this: you are enough. The love and effort you pour into your child's life are extraordinary, even if it doesn't always feel that way.

Celebrate the small victories—they are the building blocks of progress. Every step forward, no matter how small, is worth celebrating. And on the hard days, give yourself grace. It's okay to ask for help, take a break, and admit that this journey is arduous.

Remember, you are not alone in your struggles, triumphs, or questions. A whole community of parents is walking this path with you. Lean on them. Share your stories. Offer and accept support. There is power and healing in solidarity.

And most of all, remember to treasure the joy, wonder, and beauty your child brings into your life. They are not defined by their diagnosis but by their heart, spirit, and potential.

You are their greatest advocate, fiercest protector, and first home. Your love is the foundation for their success, and your unwavering belief in them is a gift they will carry forever.

You've got this. And even when you feel like you don't, know that simply showing up, loving them, and doing your best is more than enough.

With love, solidarity, and encouragement,
Dr. Simbi Animashaun

RESOURCES AND TOOLS

TIPS FOR STARTING CONVERSATIONS ABOUT AUTISM WITH OTHERS

Starting conversations about autism can feel daunting, especially when you're not sure how others will respond. Whether advocating for your child, raising awareness, or helping others understand autism, approaching the conversation with clarity, compassion, and confidence can make a big difference. Here are some tips to help you navigate these discussions:

Start with the Basics:
- Define Autism Simply: Begin with a clear and straightforward explanation. For example, "Autism is a developmental difference that affects how a person communicates, processes the world, and interacts with others. It's not a disease, just a different way of being."
- Avoid Overloading: Stick to a few key points initially to avoid overwhelming the person with too much information. For example, if someone asks, "What does autism mean?" You might respond, "It means my child experiences the world differently. They may need extra support but have strengths in some areas."

Focus on Personal Stories:
- Share Your Perspective: Personal anecdotes can be powerful and relatable. For example, "For my child, loud environments can feel overwhelming. We use noise-canceling headphones to help them feel more comfortable."

- Keep It Relatable: Help others see common ground. For example, "My child loves trains and knows everything about them—just like some kids might feel about dinosaurs or space."
- Tip: Stories personalize autism and help others understand it beyond stereotypes or clinical descriptions.

Use Positive Language:
- Highlight Strengths: Emphasize the unique qualities of autism, such as creativity, focus, or a different way of thinking.
- Avoid Deficit-Based Terms: Instead of saying, "They can't do X," frame it as "They're working on Y in their own time." Example: Instead of "They struggle to make friends," try, "They value deeper, one-on-one connections rather than big social groups."

Be Honest and Open:
- Acknowledge Challenges: It's okay to share that autism comes with joys and difficulties, which helps paint a balanced picture.
- Set Boundaries: If the conversation gets too personal, it's fine to say, "I'd rather not discuss that part, but I'm happy to talk about this instead."
- Reminder: Authenticity helps others feel comfortable asking questions or expressing their thoughts.

Use Everyday Moments as Openings:
- Casual Situations: When someone notices your child's behavior, turn it into a teaching moment. For example, if a cashier notices your child wearing headphones, you could say, "These help with loud sounds because my child is on the autism spectrum."
- Addressing Questions: Respond kindly if someone asks why your child does something differently. For example, "They're flapping their hands because they're excited—it's how they show joy!"

Tailor the Conversation to Your Audience:

- For Friends and Family, Be more detailed and personal, focusing on your child's specific needs and how they can help. For example, "If you'd like to connect with them, you could talk about dinosaurs—one of their favorite topics."
- For Strangers or Acquaintances: Keep it brief and general unless they ask follow-up questions. For example, "Autism means they process the world differently, so sometimes they need extra support."
- Tip: Adjust your approach based on how much the person already knows or wants to learn.

Encourage Questions and Curiosity:

- Invite Dialogue: Say something like, "If you're curious about autism, feel free to ask me questions—I'm happy to share."
- Address Myths: Be ready to correct misconceptions gently. For example, if someone says, "I heard vaccines cause autism," you might reply, "Actually, that's a debunked myth. Autism is something people are born with—it's part of who they are."
- Reminder: Questions show interest, so try to approach them patiently, even if they initially feel awkward.

Use Analogies to Explain Concepts:

- Analogies can make complex ideas easier to understand:
- Sensory Sensitivities: "Imagine if every sound around you felt as loud as a siren—it would be hard to concentrate, right?"
- Social Differences: "Think of it like learning a new language. Social interactions might feel like decoding unfamiliar words for someone on the spectrum.
- Tip: Tailor analogies to the listener's experiences to make the explanation resonate.

Lead with Respect and Compassion:

- Assume Good Intentions: Most people want to understand but may not know how to ask.
- Stay Calm: If someone reacts poorly or says something hurtful, try to respond with kindness. For example, "I know this is a lot to take in, but autism isn't something to fear. It's just a different way of being.
- Reminder: Your calm and respectful tone can set the tone for a productive conversation.

End on a Positive Note:

- Share a Success Story: Highlight a recent milestone or moment of joy. For example, "Last week, my child said their first full sentence—it was such an exciting moment for us!"
- Express Gratitude: Thank the person for listening or being willing to learn. For example, "I appreciate you taking the time to learn more about autism. It means a lot to families like mine."

Bonus: Tools to Help Start Conversations:

- Books and Articles: Share resources to help others understand autism. For example, "I found this book helpful in explaining autism—it might be a good starting point."
- Visual Aids: Use videos, infographics, or apps to explain concepts visually, especially for younger audiences.

Starting conversations about autism helps build understanding, reduce stigma, and create a more inclusive world for your child. You don't have to have all the answers—what matters most is your willingness to share and connect.

RECOMMENDED BOOKS, APPS, AND TOOLS FOR PARENTS AND KIDS

Here are some highly recommended books, apps, and tools for parents and children navigating the autism journey. These resources can help with understanding autism, managing challenges, fostering development, and creating connections.

Books for Parents:

"The Reason I Jump" by Naoki Higashida
- Written by a 13-year-old boy with autism, this book offers insight into how individuals on the spectrum think and feel. Its helpfulness lies in its first-person perspective on autism.

"Uniquely Human: A Different Way of Seeing Autism" by Dr. Barry M. Prizant
- Challenges conventional ideas about autism and focuses on understanding behaviors as forms of communication. Why it's helpful: Offers practical, compassionate advice for parents.

"The Out-of-Sync Child" by Carol Stock Kranowitz
- A guide to understanding sensory processing challenges often associated with autism. Why it's helpful: Provides strategies for addressing sensory sensitivities.

"Ten Things Every Child with Autism Wishes You Knew" by Ellen Notbohm
- It offers a powerful reminder of what children on the spectrum want their caregivers and educators to understand. Why it's helpful: Empathetic and empowering.

"Parenting ASD Teens: A Guide to Making It Up As You Go" by *Andrew Schlegelmilch*
- It focuses on helping parents navigate the teenage years with practical tips. Why it's helpful: Addresses a crucial and often challenging stage of development.

Books for Kids:

"All My Stripes: A Story for Children with Autism" by *Shaina Rudolph and Danielle Royer*
- It is a heartwarming story of a young zebra with autism learning to embrace his differences. Why it's helpful: Encourages self-acceptance and celebrates uniqueness.

"A Friend Like Simon" by *Kate Gaynor*
- Explores the challenges and rewards of making friends with someone on the autism spectrum. Why it's helpful: Promotes understanding and empathy among peers.

"My Brother Charlie" by *Holly Robinson Peete and Ryan Elizabeth Peete*
- A touching story about a girl's relationship with her twin brother, who has autism. Why it's helpful: It helps siblings understand and appreciate their autistic family members.

"I See Things Differently: A First Look at Autism" by *Pat Thomas*
- Introduces autism to young readers in a simple, accessible way. Why it's helpful: It is excellent for introducing the topic to classmates or friends.

"Temple Did It, and I Can Too!" by *Jennifer Gilpin Yacio*
- Inspired by the life of Temple Grandin, this book encourages kids with autism to dream big. Why it's helpful: Offers inspiration and practical advice.

Apps for Kids:

Proloquo2Go
– A highly regarded communication app for nonverbal children or those with speech delays. Why it's helpful: It enables kids to express their needs and thoughts using symbols and words.

Autism Speaks Visual Supports
– It provides customizable visual schedules and communication boards to help kids with transitions and routines. This helps improve understanding and reduce anxiety.

Endless Reader
– It focuses on building vocabulary and reading skills through interactive games. This approach is helpful because it appeals to children who learn visually or enjoy repetition.

Sensory App House (Set of Apps)
– It includes apps for sensory exploration, such as "Cause and Effect Sensory Light Box." These apps are helpful because they provide calming, interactive activities

Social Stories Creator and Library
– It helps parents create personalized social stories to teach social skills and prepare for new situations. This builds confidence and understanding.

Tools and Toys for Development:

Chewable Jewelry or Fidget Tools
– They are helpful because they provide Chewigem or Tangle Toys. Why it's helpful: It provides sensory input and helps with focus.

Weighted Blankets or Lap Pads
–   It helps children feel calm and secure during stressful moments. Why it's helpful: It offers proprioceptive input to regulate sensory systems.

Visual Schedules (e.g., PECs)
–   Picture Exchange Communication Systems help with routines and transitions. Why it's helpful: It reduces frustration by providing structure and predictability.

Noise-Canceling Headphones
–   Brands like Puro or Bose offer child-friendly versions. This is helpful because it reduces sensory overload in noisy environments.

Melissa & Doug Toys
–   Many of their puzzles and hands-on activities are great for fine motor skills. Why it's helpful: It's engaging and educational for kids on the spectrum.

Online Resources and Communities for Parents:

Autism Navigator
–   Provides online courses and resources to help parents understand autism. Why it's helpful: It's research-based and user-friendly.

Autism Speaks Resource Guide
–   Includes local resources, therapists, and support groups by region. Why it's helpful: Easy to find tailored support.

Facebook Support Groups
- Search for groups like the Autism Parents Support Group or local autism advocacy groups. Why it's helpful: Offers emotional support and practical advice from other parents.

The Mighty
- A site where parents and individuals with disabilities share stories and tips. Why it's helpful: Fosters community and understanding.

Every child and family is different so the best resources may depend on your child's needs, interests, and developmental goals. Start by exploring a few of these options and see what resonates.

A LIST OF NATIONAL AND LOCAL AUTISM SUPPORT ORGANIZATIONS

Here's a list of national and local autism support organizations that provide resources, advocacy, education, and support for families navigating autism:

National Autism Support Organizations:

Autism Society of America
- Website: https://www.autism-society.org/
- Offers support, advocacy, and resources for individuals and families. Local Chapters are available across the U.S.

Autism Speaks
- Website: https://www.autismspeaks.org/
- Provides toolkits, research funding, advocacy, and resources for individuals on the spectrum and their families.

National Autism Association (NAA)
- Website: https://www.nationalautismassociation.org/
- Focuses on safety, advocacy, and support for families, including resources for wandering prevention and crisis support.

Organization for Autism Research (OAR)
- Website: https://researchautism.org/
- Offers evidence-based information, tools, and scholarships for individuals with autism and their families.

The Arc
— Website: https://thearc.org/
— Advocates for individuals with developmental abilities, including autism, offering local Chapter support and resources.

SPARK for Autism
— Website: https://www.sparkforautism.org/
— A research initiative connecting families to autism studies and providing resources to understand autism better.

Easterseals
— Website: https://www.easterseals.com/
— Provides early intervention, therapy, and vocational training for individuals with disabilities, including autism.

Autistic Self Advocacy Network (ASAN)
— Website: https://autisticadvocacy.org/
— It aims to empower autistic individuals through advocacy and education led by people on the spectrum.

Autism Navigator
— Website: https://autismnavigator.com/
— Offers online courses and tools for families and professionals to support children with autism.

TACA (The Autism Community in Action)
— Website: https://tacanow.org/
— Provides resources, educational events, and parent mentorship to support autism families.

Local Autism Support Organizations
(Georgia and Lithonia Area):

Autism Society of Georgia
– Website: https://www.autismsocietyga.org/
– Provides advocacy, education, and support for individuals and families across Georgia.

The Marcus Autism Center (Atlanta, GA)
– Website: https://www.marcus.org/
– Offers diagnosis, therapy, and support services for children with autism and their families.

FOCUS + Fragile Kids
– Website: https://focus-ga.org/
– Provides resources, respite care, and events for families of children with developmental disabilities, including autism.

Spectrum Autism Support Group (Lawrenceville, GA)
– Website: https://www.atl-spectrum.com/
– A Gwinnett County-based group offering support meetings, social skills groups, and events for families.

Parent to Parent of Georgia
– Website: https://www.p2pga.org/
– Supports parents of children with disabilities through peer mentorship, resources, and advocacy.

All About Developmental Disabilities (Atlanta, GA)
– Website: https://aadd.org/
– Offers advocacy, resources, and community programs for families of children with developmental disabilities.

The Matthew Reardon Center for Autism (Savannah, GA)
– Website: https://www.matthewreardon.org/
– Provides comprehensive services, including advocacy and therapy, for families in Georgia.

Georgia Sensory Assistance Project (GSAP)
– Website: https://www.gvs.ga.gov/
– It focuses on assisting families and children with dual sensory impairments, including autism.

DeKalb County Schools Autism Support Services
– Website: https://www.dekalbschoolsga.org/special-education/
– Offers autism-specific educational resources and support services for students in the DeKalb County area.

Dream Makers Youth Foundation (Atlanta, GA)
– Website: https://www.dmyf.info/
– Provides respite care, social skills groups, and advocacy for children with autism and their families.

Finding Additional Local Organizations:
– Check local community centers, churches, or schools for autism support groups or events.
– Contact Parent to Parent of Georgia for a tailored list of resources near Lithonia.
– Explore Facebook groups or Meetup.com for parent-led support groups.

GLOSSARY

Here's a glossary of important terms related to autism and caregiving that may be helpful for parents, caregivers, and educators.

504 Plan:
- Provides accommodations for students with disabilities to ensure equal access to education, but without specialized instruction.

A

Americans with Disabilities Act (ADA):
- U.S. law ensures equal rights and access for individuals with disabilities.

Applied Behavior Analysis (ABA):
- A therapy based on principles of learning and behavior to teach skills and reduce challenging behaviors.

Autism Spectrum Disorder (ASD):
- A developmental disorder characterized by differences in communication, behavior, and sensory processing.

Augmentative and Alternative Communication (AAC):
- Tools or strategies (e.g., communication boards, apps) that help individuals who have difficulty speaking.

B

Behavior Intervention Plan (BIP):
- A plan created to address specific behavioral challenges is often used in schools or therapy.

Burnout:
- Physical and emotional exhaustion experienced by caregivers from prolonged stress and caregiving responsibilities.

C

Comorbidities:
- Medical or psychological conditions that occur alongside autism, such as anxiety, ADHD, or epilepsy.

Cues:
- Prompts or signals (verbal or nonverbal) that help a child understand what is expected of them.

D

Developmental Delay:
- When a child does not reach developmental milestones at the expected age.

Developmental, Individual Difference, Relationship-Based (DIR Model):
- It focuses on building relationships and fostering emotional and social development through play.

DSM-5:
- The fifth edition of the Diagnostic and Statistical Manual of Mental Disorders outlines the criteria for diagnosing ASD.

E

Early Intervention (EI):
- Programs or therapies provided to children (ages 0–3) to address developmental delays as early as possible.

Executive Functioning:
- Cognitive skills that involve planning, organization, problem-solving, and emotional regulation are often impacted by autism.

F

Floortime Therapy:
- A play-based therapy that encourages communication and emotional connection by following the child's lead.

Functional Communication:
- Therapy for nonverbal children often focuses on the ability to express wants, needs, and thoughts in a way that others understand.

H

High-Functioning Autism:
- It is a term used to describe individuals on the autism spectrum with fewer support needs (though this term is becoming less common due to its oversimplification).

Hyperfixation:
- A deep and focused interest in a specific topic or activity is common in individuals on the spectrum.

I

Identity-First Language:
- It puts the diagnosis first to embrace it as part of one's identity (e.g., "autistic person").

Individualized Education Program (IEP):
- A customized plan is developed for students with disabilities to ensure they receive appropriate support and accommodations in school.

Inclusion:
- Educating children with disabilities alongside their typically developing peers in a mainstream classroom.

Intervention:
– Any program, therapy, or strategy to improve specific skills or behaviors.

M

Meltdown:
– An intense response to overwhelming sensory or emotional input differs from a tantrum as it is not purposeful.

Motor Planning:
– The ability to plan and execute physical movements is often a challenge for individuals with autism.

N

Neurodiversity:
– A perspective that views neurological differences (e.g., autism, ADHD) as variations in the human brain rather than deficits.

Non-Verbal:
– This term refers to individuals who do not use spoken language but may communicate through gestures, sign language, pictures, or technology.

O

Occupational Therapy (OT):
– It helps individuals develop skills for daily life, such as dressing, eating, or writing, with a focus on sensory needs.

P

Picture Exchange Communication System (PECS):
– A communication tool where individuals use pictures to express their needs or thoughts.

Perseveration:
– Repeating words, phrases, or actions is often seen as a coping or self-soothing mechanism.

Person-First Language:
– Refers to the individual before the diagnosis (e.g., "person with autism").

Prompting:
– Providing cues or assistance to help a child complete a task or learn a skill.

Proprioception:
– Awareness of body position and movement; challenges in this area are common in autism.

R

Reinforcement:
– A strategy to encourage desired behavior by offering a reward or positive feedback.

Respite Care:
– Temporary care is provided to relieve primary caregivers.

Rituals/Routines:
– Predictable patterns that provide comfort and structure for individuals with autism.

S

Self-Advocacy:
– The ability to understand and communicate one's own needs and preferences.

Self-Stimulatory Behavior (Stimming):
–   Repetitive movements or sounds (e.g., flapping hands, rocking) are used to self-regulate emotions or sensory input.

Sensory Diet:
–   A personalized plan of activities designed to help an individual regulate their sensory input.

Sensory Integration Therapy:
–   It helps individuals with sensory processing challenges manage their responses to sensory stimuli.

Sensory Overload:
–   When sensory input (e.g., bright lights and loud noises) becomes overwhelming, it often leads to a meltdown.

Sensory Processing Disorder (SPD):
–   A condition where the brain has difficulty receiving and responding to sensory information is common in individuals with autism.

Speech and Language Therapy (SLT):
–   Supports communication skills, including speech, language understanding, and alternative communication methods.

Social Skills Training:
–   Therapy teaches individuals how to interact appropriately in social situations.

Social Story:
–   A short story designed to teach social skills or prepare for specific situations.

Special Education:
- Educational programs are designed to meet the needs of students with disabilities.

T

Transition:
- The process of moving from one activity, environment, or stage of life to another is often challenging for individuals with autism.

Therapy:
- Services such as speech, occupational, or physical therapy to support development and skill-building.

Token Economy:
- A behavior management system that uses tokens as rewards for desired behaviors, which the child can later exchange for a prize or privilege.

V

Vestibular System:
Related –   to balance and spatial orientation, activities like spinning or swinging can help regulate this system.

Visual Schedule:
- A tool that uses pictures or symbols to show the sequence of activities, helping individuals understand daily routines.

REFERENCES

5 Positive Ways to Handle Grief After a Loved One Passed Away | Mostly Amélie. https://mostlyamelie.com/5-ways-to-handle-grief-after-a-loved-ones-passing/

Autism Risk: Assessing Your Child's Chances - Our World And Autism. https://ourworldandautism.com/advice/chances-of-having-a-child-with-autism/

A Mother's Instinct - Southwest Autism Research & Resource Center (SARRC). https://autismcenter.org/a-mothers-instinct

Cerebral Palsy in Child: overview –   Health32. https://www.health32.com/cerebral-palsy-in-child-overview/

Chen, P. (2015). Service Delivery to Bilingual Mandarin and English Children: The Role of Speech-Language Pathologists and Parents. https://core.ac.uk/download/pdf/48496783.pdf

Chicago Feeding Group. https://chicagofeedinggroup.org/view/directory/

Daoust, P. Y., Arsenault, P., Ortenburger, A., McAlpine, D., Reid, G., & Wimmer, T. (2022). Osseous Anomalies in a Risso's Dolphin (Grampus griseus). Aquatic Mammals, 48(1), 83-91.

Expressive Aphasia - Goally. https://getgoally.com/blog/neurodiversopedia/expressive-aphasia/

Gifted/Talented Evaluations Archives - NeuroPsych Doctor. https://neuropsychdoctor.com/blog/category/gifted-talented-evaluations/

IDEA Part C | Office of Developmental Primary Care. https://odpc.ucsf.edu/communications-paper/idea-part-c

Inclusion: A Parent's Perspective - Psyched Services. https://blog.psychedservices.com/inclusion-benefits-includers-a-parents-perspective

Kingdom Team | Shepherd Church. https://shepherdchurch.com/page/2178?GroupId=1061117

Rokhim, R. F. (2022). Analysis of language disorder of the autistic savant character in The Good Doctor series movie. https://core.ac.uk/download/541111558.pdf

Shetzler, C. L. (2024). Occupational therapy coaching of the childcare provider in early childhood mental wellness. https://open.bu.edu/bitstream/2144/47909/6/Shetzler_bu_0017E_18692.pdf

Tips for Navigating Shame and Guilt in Autism Parenting | Positive Behavior Services, Inc.. https://positivebehaviorservices.com/tips-for-navigating-shame-and-guilt-in-autism-parenting/

ABOUT THE AUTHOR

Dr. Simbi Animashaun is a dedicated advocate for autism awareness and a passionate supporter of underserved families navigating the autism spectrum. With over 15 years of experience in education, Dr. Animashaun has worked tirelessly to bridge gaps in care and provide equitable resources to empower families and children.

As co-founder of Horizon Over the Spectrum, Inc., Dr. Animashaun is committed to fostering understanding, creating inclusive opportunities, and celebrating every child's unique potential. She specializes in culturally responsive approaches to autism support and ensures that families, particularly those in Black and underserved communities, receive the tools and guidance they need to thrive.

Dr. Animashaun holds an EdD in Educational Techology from Walden University. Her dissertation, *Special Educators' Experiences with Professional Development and Implementation Support in Using Digital Social Stories for Students with Autism*, is published in Proquest. When she's not advocating for mothers, children, and families, Dr. Animashaun enjoys spending time with her children, reading books, shopping, cooking, and watching classic movies.

CONTACT US

Horizon Over the Spectrum, Inc.
Email: info@horizonsoverthespectrum.com
Phone: (404) 884-8391
Website: www.horizonsoverthespectrum.com
Follow us:
- Facebook: @HorizonOverTheAutism
- Instagram: @HorizonOverTheAutism
For donations and resources,
visit: www.horizonsoverthespectrum.org/donate